James '**Jimmy**' Peter **Greaves** MBE, born on 20th February 1940, in Manor Park, east London, England, UK then brought up in Hainault, Essex was a professional footballer who played as a forward. He's England's 4th-highest international goalscorer with 44, including a record 6 hat-tricks, Tottenham Hotspur's highest scorer with 266, and the highest scorer in th with 357 goals. He finished as the 1st Division's top scorer in 6 English Football Hall of Fame.

Jimmy began his professional career at Chelsea during 1957 th Youth Cup final. He scored 124 First Division goals in just 4 sea for £80,000 in April 1961. His time in Italy wasn't happy, so he Hotspur for £99,999 in December 1961. Whilst playing for Spu then 1966–67, the Charity Shield in 1962 & 1967, plus the Euro

63, the year that Greaves came closest to winning a league title, as Tottenham were runners-up. He moved to West Ham Utd in a player-exchange in March 1970 then retired the following year. After 4-years away from the sport he returned to football at the non-league level, despite his alcoholism. During a 5-year spell he played for Brentwood, Chelmsford City, Barnet, and Woodford Town before permanently retiring from the game during 1980.

Jimmy scored 13 goals in 12 England under-23 internationals followed by 44 goals during 57 full England internationals from 1959 - 1967. He played in the 1962 & 1966 FIFA World Cup finals, but was injured in the group stage of the 1966 World Cup, losing his 1st team place to Geoff Hurst, who kept Greaves out of the first team in the final. Although England lifted the World Cup, Jimmy wasn't given a winners medal until a change of FIFA rules during 2009. He was also part of the squad that came 3rd in UEFA Euro 1968, although he didn't play in the finals.

Following his retirement as a player he went on to have a successful career in broadcasting, working alongside Ian St John on Saint and Greavsie from 1985 to 1992, while also making regular appearances on TV-am during that period. Jimmy worked on several other sport programmes on ITV including Sporting Triangles from 1987–1990.

Club career

First Division Goals in England

| Player | Goals | Matches | Goals/Matches |
|---|---|---|---|
| Jimmy Greaves | 357 | 516 | 0.69 |
| Steve Bloomer | 314 | 535 | 0.59 |
| Dixie Dean | 310 | 362 | 0.86 |
| Gordon Hodgson | 287 | 455 | 0.63 |
| Alan Shearer | 283 | 559 | 0.51 |

Greaves was scouted for Chelsea playing schoolboy football by Jimmy Thompson then was signed on as an apprentice in 1955, becoming one of 'Drake's Ducklings', named after manager Ted Drake inspired by Man. Utd's 'Busby Babes'. He soon made a big impression at youth level, scoring 51 goals during the 1955–56 season then 122 goals in the 1956–57 season under the wing of youth team coach Dick Foss. Jimmy scored in the FA Youth Cup final of 1958, but Chelsea lost the 2-legged tie 7–6 on aggregate after Wolverhampton Wanderers turned around a 4-goal deficit with a 6–1 win in the 2nd leg. He turned professional during the summer of 1957, although he spent 8 weeks working at a steel company to top up his income during the summer break.

Greaves scored for Chelsea on his 1st Division debut at the age of 17 on 24th August 1957, against Tottenham Hotspur in a 1-1 draw at White Hart Lane. The News Chronicle stated that he 'showed the ball control, confidence & positional strength of a seasoned campaigner', comparing his debut to the impact that Duncan Edwards had as a teenager. The 'Blues' played attacking football during the 1957-58 season, leading to high-scoring matches, with Jimmy ending the season as the club's top scorer with 22 goals from 37 appearances. Ted rested him for 6 weeks from mid-November as he didn't want the praise that Greaves was receiving to go to his head. Jimmy returned to the first team at Stamford Bridge with 4 goals in a 7-4 victory over Portsmouth on Christmas Day.

He scored 5 goals in a 6-2 win against league champions Wolverhampton Wanderers in the 3rd match of the season of 1958-59 but Chelsea were inconsistent, finishing in 14th place. However, Greaves ended the season as the First Division's top scorer with 32 goals from 44 league games. He scored 29 goals in 40 league matches in the 1959-60 campaign, 5 of which were in a 5-4 victory over Preston North End but the club only came 18th, three places and 3 pts above the relegation zone.

Jimmy scored hat-tricks against Wolves, Blackburn Rovers & Man. City during the 1960-61 season, having netted 4 goals against Newcastle Utd. and Nottingham Forest plus 5 goals in a 7-1 win over West Bromwich Albion. His hat-trick against Man. City on 19th November included his 100th league goal, making him the youngest player to pass the milestone, at the age of 20 years, 290 days. Despite this achievement, Greaves became disillusioned with Chelsea as the team conceded a lot of goals, never being consistent enough for a serious title challenge.

They were knocked out of the FA Cup, losing 2-1 at home to 4th Division side Crewe Alexandra then Club chairman Joe Mears agreed to sell him. Jimmy's last match for the 'Blues' was the final game of the season on 29th April 1961, when he was made captain for the day, scoring his 13th hat-trick for Chelsea, netting all their goals in a 4-3 win against Nottingham Forest. It took his total for the season to a club record 41 goals in 40 league games, as the division's top scorer & Chelsea's 2nd highest goalscorer with 132 goals.

Greaves was signed by Italian Serie A club A.C. Milan in June 1961 for £80,000, being given a 3-year contract of £140 / week with a £15,000 signing on bonus. He was unhappy at the thought of leaving London, trying to cancel the move before it was fully confirmed, but 'Rossoneri' manager Giuseppe Viani refused to drop the deal. Jimmy scored on his debut in a 2-2 draw with Botafogo at the San Siro stadium but he didn't get on well with new head coach Nereo Rocco, who insisted on keeping his players on a strict training regime with little personal freedom.

Greaves scored 9 goals from 14 appearances, including one against Inter Milan in the local derby. He kicked a player who'd spat in his face during a match against Sampdoria, who equalised from the resulting free kick, for which Rocco blamed Jimmy, despite him having scored A.C. Milan's opener then set up their 2nd. Greaves was transfer-listed because of his low morale, with Brazilian striker Dino Sani being signed as his replacement. Spurs and Chelsea made £96,500 offers, which were accepted. After he left, A.C. Milan went on to win the league title at the end of the 1961-62 season.

Bill Nicholson signed Jimmy for Tottenham during December 1961 for £99,999 following lengthy negotiations, the fee being intended to avoid the pressure of him being the first £100,000 player in British football. He joined Spurs just after they became the 1st English club to complete the First Division & FA Cup double during the 20th century. Greaves played his 1st game in a Spurs shirt for the reserve team on 9th December 1961 netting twice in a 4-1 win over Plymouth Argyle Reserves at Home Park.

He scored a hat-trick on his 1st team debut, including a flying scissor kick, in a 5-2 victory over Blackpool at White Hart Lane, going on to play against Benfica in the semi-finals of the European Cup; in the 1st leg at the Estádio da Luz Jimmy had a goal disallowed for offside then another disallowed in the return fixture for the same reason. He played in all 7 games of the club's FA Cup run, scoring 9 goals as they beat Birmingham City after a replay, Plymouth Argyle, West Bromwich Albion, Aston Villa and Manchester Utd. to reach the FA Cup Final of 1962 against Burnley at Wembley. Greaves opened the scoring against Burnley after 3 mins when he hit a low shot past goalkeeper Adam Blacklaw from a tight angle, Spurs going on to win the game 3–1.

Tottenham finished in 3rd place in the league at the end of the 1961–62 season, 4 points behind champions Ipswich Town. Jimmy scored twice in the FA Charity Shield of 1962, as Spurs lifted the trophy with a 5–1 win over Ipswich at Portman Road. During the following season he scored hat-tricks in wins over Man. Utd, Ipswich Town & Liverpool, as well as 4 goals in a 9–2 thrashing of Nottingham Forest. Spurs finished their league campaign of 1962–63 as runners-up, 6 pts behind champions Everton, Greaves having scored 37 goals in 41 league games, finishing as the top flight's top scorer.

In the European Cup Winners' Cup, Tottenham beat Glasgow Rangers, ŠK Slovan Bratislava of Czechoslovakia then OFK Beograd of Yugoslavia to reach the final, where they met Spanish club Atlético Madrid at De Kuip. In the 1st leg of the semi-final against Beograd in Belgrade, Jimmy was sent off for violent conduct, his only dismissal ever, after trying to punch centre-back Blagomir Krivokuća. He was banned for one match so was able to play in the final, where he opened the scoring after a pass from Cliff Jones, later adding a 4th in a 5–1 triumph, John White and Terry Dyson getting the other goals. In winning the competition, Tottenham became the 1st British team to lift a European trophy.

Manager Bill Nicholson and his assistant Eddie Baily then began a period of transition at White Hart Lane – Danny Blanchflower retiring aged 38 during 1964, with John White being killed by a lightning strike. Dave Mackay stayed until 1968, while Greaves remained a consistent prolific goalscorer. In the season of 1963–64 he scored hat-tricks in wins over Nottingham Forest, Blackpool, Birmingham City & Blackburn Rovers. Spurs finished in 4th place, 6 pts behind champions Liverpool, being knocked out of the FA Cup and Cup Winners' Cup at the opening stages. Jimmy netted 35 goals in 41 league games to again finish as the division's top scorer. His strike partner Bobby Smith left the club during the summer, although Greaves thought that the partnership he went on to form with new signing Alan Gilzean was even more effective.

Spurs finished 6th following the season of 1964–65, Jimmy netting 29 times in 41 league games to finish as the 1st division's joint top scorer with Andy McEvoy. He also had a couple of hat-tricks in the FA Cup, vs Torquay Utd. & Ipswich Town, taking his tally to 35 goals in 45 appearances. He missed 3 months at the start of the following season after being diagnosed with hepatitis, but recovered to end the campaign of 1965–66 with 16 goals in 31 matches, remaining the club's top scorer as they finished in 8th place in the league, having reached the 5th Round of the FA Cup.

Greaves netted 31 goals in 47 appearances during the season of 1966–67, helping Tottenham to mount a title challenge that ended with a 3rd-place finish, 4 points behind Man. Utd. They also won the FA Cup, knocking out Millwall, Portsmouth, Bristol City, Birmingham City and Nottingham Forest to reach the FA Cup Final of 1967, where Spurs faced Chelsea. Although he didn't score in the final, a 2–1 victory, with 6 goals in 8 games Jimmy was the competition's leading scorer.

The season of 1967–68 was a disappointing one for Tottenham, following their 3–3 draw with Man. Utd at Old Trafford in the FA Charity Shield of 1967. They finished 7th in the league, being knocked out of the FA Cup in the 5th Round, having exited the Cup Winners' Cup in the 2nd Round. Jimmy had a poor season by his own high standards, although with 29 goals in 48 appearances he was still the club's top scorer. Nicholson bought him a new strike partner, Martin Chivers from Southampton for a club record £125,000 transfer fee, with Alan Gilzean dropping further back into midfield, but Greaves and Chivers weren't as effective together as Bill had hoped.

Jimmy scored 27 goals in 42 league games during the season of 1968–69, finishing as the 1st Division's leading scorer for the 6th & final time. He scored 4 goals in a match against Sunderland, also getting hat-tricks against Burnley and Leicester City. His 9 goals in cup competitions, including a hat-trick against Exeter City, gave him a tally of 36 in 52 games. His goals that season took Greaves past Bobby Smith as Spurs' top goalscorer, as well as moving ahead of Steve Bloomer as the 1st Division's top scorer with 336 goals.

Spurs were inconsistent during the 1969–70 campaign, with Jimmy being dropped from the first team after an FA Cup defeat by Crystal Palace at Selhurst Park on 28th January 1970. He was never recalled to the starting line-up, but still ended the season as the club's joint top scorer with Martin Chivers, having netted 11 goals in 33 matches, taking his total to a club record 266 goals, including 15 hat-tricks, also a club record. Greaves was given a testimonial match by Spurs on 17th October 1972, a 2–1 win over Feyenoord at White Hart Lane attended by over 45,000 fans.

Jimmy joined West Ham Utd in March 1970, as part-exchange in Martin Peters' transfer to White Hart Lane. Brian Clough's Derby County had also been interested in him but he didn't want to move away from London. With hindsight Greaves thought that Clough might've helped him revive his career, as he'd done for his former Tottenham team-mate Dave Mackay, later saying that he regretted going to Upton Park. Jimmy scored 2 goals on his debut for the 'Hammers' on 21st March '70, in a 5–1 win over Man. City at Maine Road.

With Bobby Moore, Brian Dear & Clyde Best, Greaves was involved in late-night drinking during January 1971, against the instructions of manager Ron Greenwood, before a FA Cup tie away at Blackpool. On arriving in the town, Jimmy and his team-mates had been informed by members of the press that the game, scheduled for the following day, was unlikely to go ahead due to a frozen pitch. Thus, in the belief that there'd be no match the following day, Greaves drank 12 lagers in a club owned by Brian London, not returning to the team hotel until 1.45am. However, the game went ahead with West Ham losing 4–0. Jimmy stated that the defeat wasn't due to the late night, the drinking or the frozen pitch, but because the 'Hammers' team wasn't good enough. The players involved were then fined & dropped by the club.

Greaves was struggling with his fitness, believing that he'd become a journeyman footballer, having lost motivation as he thought that apart from Moore, Geoff Hurst, Billy Bonds and Pop Robson, few of his team-mates could play very well. Towards the end of his career with West Ham Jimmy began to increasingly turn to drink, often going straight from training in Chadwell Heath to a pub in Romford, where he'd stay until closing time, later accepting that he was in the early stages of alcoholism. His final game was on 1st May 1971, a 1–0 home defeat to Huddersfield Town. Greaves scored 13 goals in 40 games for West Ham, his final season in the First Division taking his tally to a record 357 goals in the top flight. Together with the 9 goals at A.C. Milan, he'd scored 366 goals in the top 5 European leagues, a record that lasted until 2017 when it was beaten by Cristiano Ronaldo.

Jimmy put on weight after leaving the 'Hammers', not attending football matches as either a player or a spectator for a couple of years. Drinking became a large part of his life, as he became an alcoholic; sometimes downing 20 pints of lager during the day then putting away a bottle of vodka in the evening, later stating that he was also regularly drunk driving during this period. While away from the game, Greaves ran for election to the London Borough of Havering as a Tory Party candidate for the Hylands ward in 1974, being narrowly defeated. Looking to overcome his alcoholism, he decided to return to football at a lower level, where he wouldn't need to be as fit as playing in the Football League. He started playing for his local side, Brentwood, making his debut on 27th December 1975 in a 2–0 loss to Witham Town.

Jimmy's return to football was successful enough to be signed for Chelmsford City of the Southern League for the season of 1976–77. He played for the club for only a few months, but their foray into the Anglo-Italian Cup, was a 'highlight' of his time there. He was still struggling with alcoholism & delirium tremens, having sought out help from Alcoholics Anonymous, following a stay in the alcoholics' ward of Warley Psychiatric Hospital.

By August 1977, still suffering from alcoholism, Greaves made his debut for Barnet in a 3–2 win against Atherstone Town. Playing from midfield during the season of 1977–78, he netted 25 goals, including 13 in the Southern League, being named their player of the season. He decided to leave the Bees early in the season of 1978–79 to focus on business interests and beating his alcoholism, despite manager Barry Fry's attempts to persuade him to stay at Underhill. Jimmy went on to make several appearances for semi-professional side Woodford Town before retiring, by which time he was sober, remaining so for the rest of his life.

## International career

### Goals for England

| Player | Goals | Matches | Goals/Match |
|---|---|---|---|
| Wayne Rooney | 53 | 120 | 0.44 |
| Bobby Charlton | 49 | 106 | 0.46 |
| Gary Lineker | 48 | 80 | 0.60 |
| Jimmy Greaves | 44 | 57 | 0.77 |
| Harry Kane | 41 | 64 | 0.64 |

Greaves made his debut for the England under-23 team in a 6–2 win over Bulgaria at Stamford Bridge on 25th September 1957, scored a couple of goals, missing out on a hat-trick after failing to convert a penalty. Jimmy won his first England cap on 17th May 1959 against Peru at the Estadio Nacional, scoring England's only goal in a 4–1 loss. The tour of the American continents was unsuccessful, England also going down to Brazil and Mexico, but Greaves escaped much criticism in the press as he was still a teenager who'd shown promise with his performances.

He netted successive hat-tricks during 1960 on 8th October then 19th October, in wins over Northern Ireland & Luxembourg. Jimmy scored another hat-trick the following year in a 9–3 thrashing of Scotland at Wembley on 15th April 1961, having a 4th goal ruled out for offside. He played in all 4 of England's games at the FIFA World Cup finals of 1962 in Chile, scoring a goal in the 3–1 win over Argentina before playing in their quarter-final loss to Brazil. During the defeat to Brazil a stray dog ran onto the pitch, evading all of the players' efforts to catch it until Greaves got down on all 4s to beckon to the animal, which the Brazilian player Garrincha thought was so funny that he took it home as a pet.

He netted 4 goals in an 8–3 trouncing of Northern Ireland on 20th November 1963 then scored another hat-trick against the same team on 3rd October of the following year making Jimmy England's all-time top goalscorer with 35 goals. He struck 4 goals again on 29th June 1966, in a 6–1 friendly win over Norway, taking his tally to 43 goals while making sure of a starting place in the FIFA World Cup finals of 1966.

At the World Cup he played in all 3 group games against Uruguay, Mexico and France, but in the win over France, midfielder Joseph Bonnel raked his studs down Greaves' shin, causing a wound that required 14 stitches, leaving a permanent scar. His replacement for the quarter-final vs Argentina, Geoff Hurst, scored the only goal of the game, keeping his place all the way to the final, when he scored a hat-trick as England won the World Cup.

Jimmy was fit to play in the final, but manager Alf Ramsey decided against changing a winning team. He was bitterly disappointed to have missed the World Cup final, stating: "I danced around the pitch with everyone else but even in this moment of triumph and great happiness, deep down I felt my sadness. Throughout my years as a professional footballer I'd dreamed of playing in a World Cup Final. I'd missed out on the match of a lifetime & it hurt".

Only the 11 players on the pitch at the end of the 4–2 win over West Germany received medals but following a Football Association-led campaign to persuade FIFA to award medals to all the winners' squad members, Greaves was presented with his medal by Prime Minister Gordon Brown at a ceremony at 10 Downing Street on 10th June 2009. During November 2014, Jimmy's medal was sold at auction for £44,000.

He played only 3 more times for England after the World Cup of 1966, scoring just 1 more goal, his final cap coming in a 1–0 victory over Austria on 27th May 1967. He was England's all-time top goalscorer, having netted 44 goals during 57 appearances, being overhauled the following year by Bobby Charlton. Although Greaves was called up for UEFA Euro 1968, he was an unused substitute throughout the tournament, as the team finished in 3rd place then retired from international football early the following year after telling Alf that he'd no intention of becoming a bit-part player in the England squad. Jimmy had dropped to 4th place on the all-time list of England goalscorers when he passed away, behind Wayne Rooney, Bobby Charlton and Gary Lineker but still held the record for most hat-tricks for England, with 6.

Greaves was a prolific goalscorer, saying that his relaxed attitude was the reason for his assured composure & confidence. He had great acceleration and pace, as well as great positional skills, clinical finishing, and opportunism inside the penalty area, also being a great dribbler.

Jimmy became a columnist for The Sun newspaper in 1979, continuing to write for it until 2009, when he began working as a columnist for The Sunday People. He worked as a pundit on Star Soccer from 1980, before later co-presenting The Saturday Show then chosen as a pundit for ITV's coverage of the FIFA World Cup of 1982. This led to his work on World of Sport & On the Ball, on which he formed a very popular partnership with Ian St John. Greg Dyke also hired Greaves to work as a TV reviewer and presenter on TV-am, which he stated was a way of 'dumbing down' the programme to attract more viewers.

Jimmy & Ian St. John presented the Saturday lunchtime football programme Saint and Greavsie From October 1985 to April 1992. He went on to work as a team captain on Sporting Triangles, opposite Andy Gray & Emlyn Hughes. Jimmy's TV career was curtailed as the Premier League was starting up, which he believed was because his light-hearted approach to football wasn't regarded as serious enough for TV bosses. However, he continued as a pundit at Central Television until 1998. He published his autobiography, Greavsie, during 2003, having also written many books in partnership with his lifelong friend, the journalist and author Norman Giller.

Jimmy wed Irene Barden at Romford register office on 26th March 1958 & although the couple began a divorce process during the depths of his alcoholism, it was never finalised before they reunited after 3 months apart. The couple renewed their vows on 7th September 2017 in Danbury, Essex. They had 5 children; Jimmy Jr, who died before his 1st birthday in 1960, Lynn (born 1959), Mitzi (born 1962), Andrew (born 1965), and Danny (born 1963), who was a professional footballer with Southend United.

Greaves took out a £1,000 bank loan whilst playing for Tottenham Hotspur to start a packing business with his brother-in-law, which by the end of his playing career had an annual turnover of over £1 million. He had a number of other business interests, including a travel agency. Jimmy entered the London to Mexico World Cup Rally of 1970, his 1st ever rally, alongside co-driver, Tony Fall, driving a Ford Escort to finish $6^{th}$ of the 96 entrants.

Greaves had surgery on an artery in his neck following a mild stroke in February 2012 then following a full recovery, he had a severe stroke during May 2015, which left him unable to speak. He was put in intensive care but was expected by doctors to slowly recover, being discharged from hospital a month later, when his friend & agent, Terry Baker, said his health had "improved considerably". Jimmy was still recovering slowly from his stroke with the use of a wheelchair by February 2016, after he'd been told that he'd never walk again. Greaves was made a Member of the Order of the British Empire (MBE) in the New Year Honours list of 2021, along with fellow World Cup of 1966 winning squad member, Ron Flowers, for their services to football. The pair were the last surviving England players from the tournament to be honoured by Queen Elizabeth II.

Jimmy Greaves died at his home in Danbury on 19th September 2021, at the age of 81. His passing coincided with the Premier League match between Tottenham and Chelsea, the 2 main clubs that he played for, with a minute of applause honouring his memory.

Career statistics

Club

Appearances & goals by club, season and competition

| Club | Season | Division | League | | FA Cup | | League Cup | | Other | | Total | |
|---|---|---|---|---|---|---|---|---|---|---|---|---|
| | | | Apps | Goals | Apps | Goals | Apps | Goals | Apps | Goals | Apps | Goals |
| London XI | 1955–58 | Non league | 0 | 0 | 0 | 0 | 0 | 0 | 2 | 2 | 2 | 2 |
| Chelsea | 1957–58 | 1st Division | 35 | 22 | 2 | 0 | 0 | 0 | 0 | 0 | 37 | 22 |
| | 1958–59 | 1st Division | 42 | 32 | 2 | 2 | 0 | 0 | 3 | 3 | 47 | 37 |
| | 1959–60 | 1st Division | 40 | 29 | 2 | 1 | 0 | 0 | 0 | 0 | 42 | 30 |
| | 1960–61 | 1st Division | 40 | 41 | 1 | 0 | 2 | 2 | 0 | 0 | 43 | 43 |
| | Total | | 157 | 124 | 7 | 3 | 2 | 2 | 3 | 3 | 169 | 132 |
| A.C. Milan | 1961–62 | Serie A | 12 | 9 | 2 | 0 | 0 | 0 | 0 | 0 | 14 | 9 |
| Tottenham Hotspur | | | | | | | | | | | | |
| | 1961–62 | 1st Division | 22 | 21 | 7 | 9 | 0 | 0 | 2 | 0 | 31 | 30 |
| | 1962–63 | 1st Division | 41 | 37 | 1 | 0 | 0 | 0 | 7 | 7 | 49 | 44 |
| | 1963–64 | 1st Division | 41 | 35 | 2 | 0 | 0 | 0 | 2 | 1 | 45 | 36 |
| | 1964–65 | 1st Division | 41 | 29 | 4 | 6 | 0 | 0 | 0 | 0 | 45 | 35 |
| | 1965–66 | 1st Division | 29 | 15 | 2 | 1 | 0 | 0 | 0 | 0 | 31 | 16 |
| | 1966–67 | 1st Division | 38 | 25 | 8 | 6 | 1 | 0 | 0 | 0 | 47 | 31 |
| | 1967–68 | 1st Division | 39 | 23 | 4 | 3 | 0 | 0 | 5 | 3 | 48 | 29 |
| | 1968–69 | 1st Division | 42 | 27 | 4 | 4 | 6 | 5 | 0 | 0 | 52 | 36 |
| | 1969–70 | 1st Division | 28 | 8 | 4 | 3 | 1 | 0 | 0 | 0 | 33 | 11 |
| | Total | | 321 | 220 | 36 | 32 | 8 | 5 | 16 | 11 | 381 | 268 |
| West Ham United | | | | | | | | | | | | |
| | 1969–70 | 1st Division | 6 | 4 | 0 | 0 | 0 | 0 | 0 | 0 | 6 | 4 |
| | 1970–71 | 1st Division | 32 | 9 | 1 | 0 | 1 | 0 | 0 | 0 | 34 | 9 |
| | Total | | 38 | 13 | 1 | 0 | 1 | 0 | 0 | 0 | 40 | 13 |
| Brentwood Town | | | | | | | | | | | | |
| | 1975–76 | Essex Senior League | | | | | | | | | | |
| Chelmsford City | | Southern League Premier Division | | | | | | | | | | |
| | 1976–77 | | 38 | 20 | 0 | 0 | 0 | 0 | 0 | 0 | 38 | 20 |
| Barnet | | Southern League Premier Division | | | | | | | | | | |
| | 1977–78 | | 30 | 13 | 5 | 4 | 0 | 0 | 1 | 1 | 36 | 18 |

| | | | | | | | | | | | |
|---|---|---|---|---|---|---|---|---|---|---|---|
| | Southern League Premier Division | | | | | | | | | | |
| | 1978–79 | 21 | 3 | 6 | 3 | 0 | 0 | 1 | 1 | 28 | 7 |
| | Total | 51 | 16 | 11 | 7 | 0 | 0 | 2 | 2 | 64 | 25 |
| Woodford Town | Athenian League | | | | | | | | | | |
| | 1979–80 | | | | | | | | | | |
| | Career total | 617 | 402 | 57 | 42 | 11 | 7 | 23 | 18 | 708 | 469 |

## International

Appearances & goals for England

| Year | Apps | Goals |
|---|---|---|
| 1959 | 5 | 2 |
| 1960 | 6 | 9 |
| 1961 | 4 | 5 |
| 1962 | 10 | 6 |
| 1963 | 9 | 8 |
| 1964 | 8 | 6 |
| 1965 | 5 | 2 |
| 1966 | 7 | 5 |
| 1967 | 3 | 1 |
| Total | 57 | 44 |

International caps and goals

England's goal tally listed first.

International appearances & goals

| # | Date | Venue | Opponent | Result | Competition | Goals |
|---|---|---|---|---|---|---|
| 1959 | | | | | | |
| 1 | 17th May | Estadio Nacional, Lima | Peru | 1–4 | Friendly | 1 |
| 2 | 24th May | Estadio Olímpico Universitario, Mexico City | Mexico | 1–2 | Friendly | |
| 3 | 28th May | Wrigley Field, Los Angeles, | United States | 8–1 | Friendly | |
| 4 | 17th Oct. | Ninian Park, Cardiff | Wales | 1–1 | British Home Championship | 1 |
| 5 | 28th Oct. | Wembley Stadium, London | Sweden | 2–3 | Friendly | |
| 1960 | | | | | | |
| 6 | 11th May | Wembley Stadium, London | Yugoslavia | 3–3 | Friendly | 1 |
| 7 | 15th May | Santiago Bernabéu Stadium, Madrid | Spain | 0–3 | Friendly | |
| 8 | 8th Oct. | Windsor Park, Belfast | Northern Ireland | 5–2 | British Home Championship | 2 |
| 9 | 19th Oct. | Stade Municipale, Luxembourg | Luxembourg | 8–0 | World Cup qualifier | 3 |
| 10 | 26th Oct. | Wembley Stadium, London | Spain | 4–2 | Friendly | 1 |
| 11 | 23rd Nov. | Wembley Stadium, London | Wales | 5–1 | British Home Championship | 2 |
| 1961 | | | | | | |
| 12 | 15th Apr. | Wembley Stadium, London | Scotland | 9–3 | British Home Championship | 3 |
| 13 | 21st May | Estádio Nacional, Oeiras | Portugal | 1–1 | World Cup qualifier | |
| 14 | 24th May | Stadio Olimpico, Rome | Italy | 2–3 | Friendly | 1 |
| 15 | 27th May | Praterstadion, Vienna | Austria | 1–3 | Friendly | 1 |

## 1962

| | | | | | | | |
|---|---|---|---|---|---|---|---|
| 16 | 14th Apr. | Hampden Park, Glasgow | Scotland | 0–2 | British Home Championship | |
| 17 | 9th May | Wembley Stadium, London | Switzerland | 3–1 | Friendly | |
| 18 | 20th May | Estadio Nacional, Lima | Peru | 4–0 | Friendly | 3 |
| 19 | 31st May | Estadio Braden, Rancagua | Hungary | 1–2 | FIFA World Cup | |
| 20 | 2nd June | Estadio Braden, Rancagua | Argentina | 3–1 | FIFA World Cup | 1 |
| 21 | 7th June | Estadio Braden, Rancagua | Bulgaria | 0–0 | FIFA World Cup | |
| 22 | 10th June | Estadio Sausalito, Viña del Mar | Brazil | 1–3 | FIFA World Cup | |
| 23 | 3rd Oct. | Hillsborough Stadium, Sheffield | France | 1–1 | European Nations' Cup qual. | |
| 24 | 20th Oct. | Windsor Park, Belfast | Northern Ireland | 3–1 | British Home Championship | 1 |
| 25 | 21st Nov. | Wembley Stadium, London | Wales | 4–0 | British Home Championship | 1 |

## 1963

| | | | | | | | |
|---|---|---|---|---|---|---|---|
| 26 | 27th Feb. | Parc des Princes, Paris | France | 2–5 | European Nations' Cup qual. | |
| 27 | 6th Apr. | Wembley Stadium, London | Scotland | 1–2 | British Home Championship | |
| 28 | 8th May | Wembley Stadium, London | Brazil | 1–1 | Friendly | |
| 29 | 29th May | Tehelné pole, Bratislava | Czechoslovakia | 4–2 | Friendly | 2 |
| 30 | 5th June | St. Jakob Stadium, Basel | Switzerland | 8–1 | Friendly | |
| 31 | 12th Oct. | Ninian Park, Cardiff | Wales | 4–0 | British Home Championship | 1 |
| 32 | 23rd Oct. | Wembley Stadium | Rest of World | 2–1 | Friendly | 1 |
| 33 | 20th Nov. | Wembley Stadium | Northern Ireland | 8–3 | British Home Championship | 4 |

## 1964

| | | | | | | | |
|---|---|---|---|---|---|---|---|
| 34 | 6th May | Wembley Stadium, London | Uruguay | 2–1 | Friendly | |
| 35 | 17th May | Estádio Nacional, Lisbon | Portugal | 4–3 | Friendly | |
| 36 | 24th May | Dalymount Park, Dublin | Rep. of Ireland | 3–1 | Friendly | 1 |
| 37 | 30th May | Estádio do Maracanã, Rio de J. | Brazil | 1–5 | Taça das Nações | 1 |
| 38 | 4th June | Pacaembu Stadium, São Paulo | Portugal | 1–1 | Taça das Nações | |
| 39 | 6th June | Estádio do Maracanã, Rio de J. | Argentina | 0–1 | Taça das Nações | |
| 40 | 3rd Oct. | Windsor Park, Belfast | Northern Ireland | 4–3 | British Home Championship | 3 |
| 41 | 21st Oct. | Wembley Stadium, London | Belgium | 2–2 | Friendly | |
| 42 | 9th Dec. | Olympic Stadium, Amsterdam | Holland | 1–1 | Friendly | 1 |

## 1965

| | | | | | | | |
|---|---|---|---|---|---|---|---|
| 43 | 10th Apr. | Wembley Stadium, London | Scotland | 2–2 | British Home Championship | 1 |
| 44 | 5th May | Wembley Stadium, London | Hungary | 1–0 | Friendly | 1 |
| 45 | 9th May | Red Star Stadium, Belgrade | Yugoslavia | 1–1 | Friendly | |
| 46 | 2nd Oct. | Ninian Park, Cardiff | Wales | 0–0 | British Home Championship | |
| 47 | 20th Oct. | Wembley Stadium, London | Austria | 2–3 | Friendly | |

## 1966

| | | | | | | | |
|---|---|---|---|---|---|---|---|
| 48 | 4th May | Wembley Stadium, London | Yugoslavia | 2–0 | Friendly | 1 |
| 49 | 29th June | Ullevaal Stadion, Oslo | Norway | 6–1 | Friendly | 4 |
| 50 | 3rd July | Idrætsparken, Copenhagen | Denmark | 2–0 | Friendly | |
| 51 | 5th July | Silesian Stadium, Chorzów | Poland | 1–0 | Friendly | |
| 52 | 11th July | Wembley Stadium, London | Uruguay | 0–0 | FIFA World Cup | |
| 53 | 16th July | Wembley Stadium, London | Mexico | 2–0 | FIFA World Cup | |
| 54 | 20th July | Wembley Stadium, London | France | 2–0 | FIFA World Cup | |

## 1967

| | | | | | | | |
|---|---|---|---|---|---|---|---|
| 55 | 15th Apr. | Wembley Stadium, London | Scotland | 2–3 | British Home Championship | |
| 56 | 24th May | Wembley Stadium, London | Spain | 2–0 | Friendly | 1 |
| 57 | 27th May | Praterstadion, Vienna | Austria | 1–0 | Friendly | |

Honours

Club

Chelsea

FA Youth Cup runner-up: 1957–58

A.C. Milan

Serie A: 1961–62

Tottenham Hotspur

FA Cup: 1961–62, 1966–67
FA Charity Shield: 1962, 1967 (shared)
European Cup Winners Cup: 1962–63
Football League First Division runner-up: 1962–63


International

England

FIFA World Cup: 1966

British Home Championship (5): 1959–60 (shared), 1960–61, 1963–64 (shared), 1964–65, 1965–66; runner-up (3): 1961–62, 1962–63, 1966–67


The crowd was only slightly below that of the visit of West Ham Utd, the mood was nostalgic, the entertainment excellent, with the result predictable, even to the scorer of the 1st goal. Everything was as it should've been at White Hart Lane for the final game of Jimmy Greaves. As Spurs defeated their Dutch opponents Feyenoord 2-1 in his testimonial match the bovver boots stamped out a rhythm of approval, the chanting was warm & witty and the North Bank invited 45,000 others to join them in 'All who love Jimmy clap your hands'.

During his 15 playing years the mention of the word work-rate to Greaves brought a wince of pain, being meant for artisans, genius coming from a moment of movement. One didn't have to run like a racehorse or train like a slave; putting away a goal in the back of the net being the object of the exercise, Jimmy had said. 30 months away from the dressing rooms of White Hart Lane & a season of Sunday works football wasn't quite the best preparation for facing one of the best sides in Europe and for one of the best teams in the 1st Division but within 3 minutes of the match kicking off the old intuition was back again.

The familiar flashing movement was followed by a typical goal from Greaves, as he seized on to Perryman's pass then the old lethal left foot flicked the ball past the black-clad Reitsma, who was beaten just as 100s of goalkeepers before him. Jimmy might well have had another, there being good football to follow with Martin Chivers sharp & eager. Alan Gilzean, the latest king of White Hart Lane, was applauded for his perfectly headed passes, while there was some fine work by Coates, who was substituted later, along with Gilzean, and England.

The Dutch gave an edge of competition to the match, perhaps overdoing it. Van Daele, a tall young man who played in horn-rimmed glasses, was shown a yellow card for one of several fouls on Chivers. There was clever support from De Jong of Hasil & Vos for Ressel, who equalised for Feyenoord after 24 mins, being of the best players on the field. The Flatlanders might well have gone ahead if not for the quick reactions of Daines, getting an unexpected taste of European opposition in goal, pulling off a great save from Wery, who was later injured, being replaced by Kristensen.

Jimmy got a cheer every time he touched the ball, being unlucky when he outsmarted Rijsbergen then stabbed the ball across the face of the goal only for Reitsma to fall at the feet of Chivers. The match was decided in the last few minutes by a shot from Evans. At the end the crowd sang for Greaves, chanting "Jimmy for England", but he wouldn't be back, being seen on the Parks pitches, playing for his works side on Sunday mornings. For one of his fans the night was particularly worthwhile, having travelled up from Torquay, who won a car in a competition.

It was the biggest football scandal of the early '70s, when England's captain Bobby Moore and the game's greatest goalscorer Jimmy Greaves, were spotted in a drinking den one freezing night in Blackpool, before a big FA Cup tie. The memories flooded back nearly 40 years later when the Hammers & Blackpool faced each other at Upton Park for the 1st time since January 1971, when they played at Bloomfield Road in the FA Cup.

On that frozen New Year weekend, after a couple of drinks at their hotel, Greaves and Moore were intending having an early night when they bumped into a couple of BBC cameramen from Match of the Day. One of them told the pair that the Blackpool pitch was iced over, so it'd take a miracle for the match not to be called off. Jimmy & Bobby, Hammers' striker Brian Dear and tee-total forward Clyde Best took a cab to ex-boxer Brian London's 007 nightclub, returning to their hotel under 3 hrs later, hardly any worse for wear but they'd been spotted by West Ham supporters.

Unfortunately for the players, the 'miracle' occurred, the pitch being declared fit with the tie going ahead on a pitch like a skating rink, on which Blackpool defeated the Hammers 4-0. An irate fan phoned West Ham Utd & a newspaper then a full-blown scandal ensued. The Hammers and the FA took punitive action then Sir Alf Ramsey dropped Moore from the following month's England match against Malta. Greaves was dropped by the club, while Brian Dear & Clyde Best's careers at West Ham Utd were suddenly curtailed.

Bobby and his team mates were slated for going out before a match. Many years later, Jimmy said: "The story was plastered all over as if we'd been guilty of the crime of the century". Moore said in 1985: "It was a completely innocent couple of hours. We only drank 2 or 3 glasses of beer. Clyde Best drank orange juice. After that things were never the same between myself and West Ham. I had claret-&-blue blood, but I could never forgive the club for the way they treated me".

Jimmy Greaves was on home ground in the Holiday Inn, Brentwood, on the fringes of his beloved east London, close to his new home in Chelmsford. Everyone recognised him; a man Greaves met in the car park greeting him like an old friend; a frisson of excitement ran through a group of executives when they spotted Jimmy, who they had to shake by the hand. He didn't even have to pay for his coffee, Greavsie being royalty around there.

Old footballers could be dull but Jimmy wasn't. He'd retired over 30 years earlier, when booze was already taking its toll on his muscular physique, but Greaves preferred not to dwell on the past. Although he'd been a phenomenon, a star as big in his day as David Beckham, it had all been a long time ago and he was no prima donna. Jimmy's autobiography had just been published, ghost-written by an old pal, but infused with its subject's spirit. His twinkling eyes, liking for long French cigarettes & the high-pitched laugh that punctuated his conversation marked him out as a survivor, the Essex-man barbs aimed at Tony Blair failing to dent his geniality, being more nostalgic sorrow at a lost world than real rage at the new.

When Jimmy was a pro, wages were low, most players driving Ford Cortinas rather than Ferraris, so did he regret missing out on the bonanza that had accelerated during the '90s? "Bloody sure. Let's make no bones about it. I wish I was playing today. Some of the players get half a dozen goals a year but earn a fortune. I look back at my Chelsea days when you had to fight to get £8 / week in the winter and £7 / week in the summer, now there are players who haven't even played in the 1st team on 40 grand / week".

Greaves, whose dad drove a tube train, was born in the East End in 1940 then grew up in Dagenham. He was a leading schoolboy footballer - "At that time we were bred with football in our veins & there really wasn't anything else". Jimmy signed for Chelsea aged 15, made a sensational, goal-scoring first-team debut at 17 then became an England player aged 19. He wed at 18, having 4 kids by the age of 26 - his 1st son, Jimmy junior, died of pneumonia at 4 months old. Even by the standards of the '60s, his was life in the fast lane. "It was a 13-year career but there was no hanging about in it. I made a huge impact in my first game, and from there on, in many ways, there was only one way to go. I spent the next 13 years making sure that I didn't".

The biggest disappointment of Greaves' career was missing the World Cup final of 1966, having been touted as England's potential match-winner in the run-up to the competition, although it was his replacement, Geoff Hurst, whose hat-trick in the final sealed the triumph. Some had blamed Jimmy's subsequent alcoholism on missing out on that historic victory, but he rejected that: "A lot of folk say to me, 'You must've been devastated in '66 but I always say, 'No, I was delighted, obviously', although that really was a small part of my career.

The interesting fact about the World Cup of '66 is that when we won it, it was quite a low-key affair. If we won it now, the country would come to a stop for a week & every player would become an immediate superstar. When we won it in '66, everybody cheered, a few thousand came out to say well done, but within a week everybody had disappeared, we'd all gone on our way and we'd starting playing the next season. That was the end of it. Now you get all this aura surrounding '66, but it was never quite like that".

Footballers' careers are nearly over before they've had a chance to think about what it means, Jimmy being no different. "I don't think when you're that young that you think about tomorrow that deeply. Being young is for the living". Great for 20-somethings but less so when moving into your 30s. Greaves said that he knew too many players who'd spent their lives dwelling on the brief glories of their playing days. "It's one of the great tragedies of being a professional footballer. They shoot horses, don't they & I think that a lot of players would prefer to have been shot once their career was over, because they've found it very difficult to battle through life. A lot of them never really find a substitute for football".

Jimmy retired at 30 but wishes that he'd carried on for longer, having found the transition difficult. He started a packaging business with his brother-in-law, but missed the buzz that soccer had given him. The drinking that had dogged the latter part of his career became chronic. 'I lost the '70s completely. They passed me by. I was drunk from 1972 to 1977. I woke up one morning and realised that it was a different world. I'd been living in it, but I hadn't been aware of it'.

Greaves' autobiography contained a chilling account of his descent into alcoholism. 'On occasions I'd drink up to 20 pints of beer in the course of a day, go home then drink a whole bottle of vodka before going to bed. I couldn't go without a drink. I used to put a bottle of vodka by my bed so that I could have a few drinks as soon as I woke up. That stopped my hands shaking, steadied my nerves & set me up for another day of binge-drinking".

The booze aged him, the book depicting the transformation from superbly honed athlete in 1970 to sunken-eyed alcoholic by 1972, reduced him to bankruptcy and led his wife Irene to begin divorce proceedings. Jimmy was living in a one-bedroom flat in Wanstead, east London towards the end of the '70s, eking-out a living selling women's jumpers, before acknowledging that he'd hit rock-bottom, so had to fight back: "I realised that I had to stop drinking long before I stopped. It wasn't an overnight thing. A mile up the road from here is Warley mental home, where I spent 5 months of my last year of drinking during 1977. I spent more time in there than I spent anywhere else. It wasn't easy".

Greaves quit drinking in February 1978, saying that he hadn't had a drop since. "One day I said, 'That's it' then I just walked away from it & fortunately, to this day, I've stayed clear of it. Are there times when I really want to have a drink? Of course there are, same as everybody else; it doesn't dehumanise you. You get down the same as everybody else and you'd like to go out to have a few jars, but you know that you can't do that". He called himself a non-drinking alcoholic.

Jimmy toured theatres with another footballing alcoholic, George Best, but said that he'd never volunteer advice on how to beat booze. "George is a highly intelligent ma and I don't think you could actually tell him very much about what he's got to do & what he hasn't got to do. He's intelligent enough to realise what his situation is. Hopefully, the last little episode that he had was a blip and he's back on the right road. I'd never advise anybody on how to deal with alcoholism unless I was asked, even then I can only tell folk how I dealt with it. I can't say, 'This is what you've got to do', because they may be living in an entirely different set of circumstances".

Greaves gradually pieced his life back together once he was off the drink. He moved back in with his wife, the couple still being together, although they'd never remarried: "I've suggested it, but she's politely said, 'No, I'm quite happy with the way we are. Jimmy started a column in the Sun during 1979, which he still wrote before developing a 2nd career as a football pundit in the '80s, forming a 10-year partnership with ex Liverpool player Ian St John.

Saint and Greavsie became a TV institution - more folk remember him as a pundit than as a player - & when it was axed during 1992 it was front-page news. Jimmy reckons the chop fell prematurely: "I think there was still quite a lot of mileage in Saint and Greavsie & I was bitter at the way that it was done. For a communications industry, there's not a great deal of communication in the media when there's bad news". Football was being Hornby-ised, producers believing that the presentation of the game needed to be more sophisticated, so Jimmy, with his outspoken views, cockney humour and greying walrus moustache, was deemed surplus to requirements.

He continued as a TV pundit in the Midlands with Central TV for a few years, before that fizzled out too, as his 2nd career came to an end. However, Greaves hadn't stopped working, saying he couldn't afford to. "Playing football gave me a good living & TV also gave me a good living, but if you say, 'Have I got any money?', the answer's 'No'. I've just never earned enough to pack it away". What would he have done if he'd never kicked a ball? "I don't know what I would've been doing. A 2nd-hand car dealer, who knows? I've been a ducker and diver at times in my life", though not on the pitch: such was his talent as a goalscorer that he'd never had to take a dive.


Ron Atkinson & Gary Newbon had urged folk to pray for their friend Jimmy Greaves who was in intensive care after having a major stroke, the 75-year-old former Chelsea, Spurs and England striker being seriously ill in hospital. Jimmy, who worked for Central TV during his media career, had had a minor stroke in 2012 but made a full recovery. Ex Aston Villa manager Atkinson, aged 76, who worked alongside Greaves as a pundit on ITV, said:

"I'm really upset to hear this news. He was a great pundit. He had a wonderful sense of humour. He was best remembered for his Saint & Greavsie show which was brilliant. I worked with Jimmy and Gary Newbon & we had such a laugh together. As a footballer he was up there as one of the best. I know George Best and Dennis Law ranked him right up there as one of the best strikers of their generation. I think sometimes it may be overlooked how good he really was. He was brilliant. I really hope he can recover from this & my best wishes go out to his wife Irene and his children".

Gary Newbon was devastated to hear the news of his friend, having been instrumental in bringing Jimmy to ITV during 1980 for a football programme called Star Soccer, which ran from 1965 to 1983 focusing on Midland teams. Gary hosted the show, believing that Greaves would be perfect for the role after reading his witty column in the Sun. He said: "I suggested that he should be involved in the show, recommending him to producer Tony Flannagan. Jimmy said no at 1st but then he rang back the next day saying that his wife had persuaded him to be involved & he hoped it wasn't too late for him to be a part of the show. We agreed then he proved to be a great signing. He was a big hit with viewers and his TV career took off after that. He was a very funny man & very astute. We worked together on ITV for 18 years. I made the decision to let him go as Controller Of Sport at ITV in 1998 as we took on Andy Townsend. We lost touch for some time but met up at a funeral during 2012 and got on great again together".

Newbon, aged 71, knew only too well the perils of strokes, having suffered one himself in 2002 in a Manchester hotel, while covering a game between Man. Utd & Sunderland. He added: "I lost my speech and the ability to walk but I was fortunate as it was caught early. I was in hospital for a week & it took me 15 weeks to recover. "I made changes to my diet and my lifestyle after that. I know only too well the affects of having a stroke & Jimmy's is much more severe than mine was. I just really hope he can pull through this but it is a severe stroke.

I really respected Jimmy and loved his company. He was an alcoholic but made the decision to give up alcohol during 1979, which saved his marriage. He never touched a drop again. My thoughts are with Jimmy & his family at this time. I would urge people to pray for him and hope he can pull through". Greaves had been working regularly on the personal appearances circuit with his friend & agent Terry Baker before the stroke. He was due to be inducted into the Tottenham Hotspur Hall of Fame on May 13th at a sell-out ceremony at White Hart Lane.

How were things with Jimmy? "Fine, apart from the stroke". "You b*gger. Only you'd try to upstage me when I'm supposed to be getting all the sympathy because of my heart attack". Norman Giller was sworn to secrecy about Greaves' condition, who'd since had an operation, being back to his silver-tongued old self. Norman wouldn't have breathed a word about it, but the internet had been awash with rumours about Jimmy's health, talk of his pending demise being greatly exaggerated.

He'd soon be back hitting balls around the Essex golf club that he part owned, folk not having heard the last of his jokes as a great stand-up comedian, as normal service resumed with the biting column he co-wrote with Dave Kidd in the Sunday People. Jimmy's writing partnership with Giller that had produced 20 books by 2012, was still alive, with its 1st 'This One's On Me', remaining the best seller on 93,000 copies.

Published in 1978, it told the harrowing story of Greaves' battle to beat the bottle. The opening line was: "My name is Jimmy G, and I'm an alcoholic". Neither co-writer had touched a drop of the hard stuff since then. When they finished the book they drank a toast then said: "Let's go & get sober out of our minds". This One's On Me Revisited, would update the original, which had been ground breaking 34 years earlier, no leading sportsman or broadcaster having opened up so brutally honestly on his drink problems.

Just how good was Greavsie? For those too young to have witnessed his footballing exploits, only being aware of him as a TV celebrity - when you're watching Lionel Messi, it's like an action replay of Jimmy at his best. The way Messi ran at defences, the way he changed pace and direction & the way he finished – passing the ball into the net – was pure Greavsie. The close control was almost identical, the sudden acceleration, the ability to shoot with either foot, the same low gravity and perfect balance.

It was all a flashback to 'Our Jim', who'd scored 220 league goals by the time he was 24. Lionel had amassed 152 by that age, without being hindered by bad fouls from defenders including 'Chopper' Harris, Norman 'Bites Yer Legs' Hunter and 'Anfield Iron' Tommy Smith. YouTube held the evidence, including Jimmy's demolition of the Man. Utd defence in 1965, on the way to a goal that opened the Match of the Day titles until the arrival of colour TV.

Greaves' most dazzling goals came when he was wearing a Chelsea shirt & playing with the gay abandonment of youth. Sadly, few of his Chelsea crackers were recorded for posterity, but fans who were around back then would confirm that many of them were magical. Jimmy scored 124 league goals for Chelsea, including 3 five-goal hauls, before he was 21 then 220 league goals for Spurs before hanging up his boots by the age of 31, after netting an all-time record 357 first division goals.

There was a messianic fervour about Messi, being Jimmy Greaves with bells on, with his desire and determination to run his socks off for Barcelona. Greaves conceded that running without the ball was not something that had appealed to him, sometimes going missing for much of the match, after which the talk would usually be about his winning goal. Jimmy didn't just decorate games, he often decided them.

Lionel still had a question mark over him when it came to the international stage. When Argentina faced Venezuela he was a pale shadow of the master of Barcelona. It seemed that he didn't know whether his role was schemer or striker, falling between the 2, having scored only 19 goals in 66 internationals. Greaves record for England was 44 goals from 57 internationals, 5 short of Bobby Charlton's record of 49 goals in 106 games.

There were still those who thought Alf Ramsey was crazy to leave Jimmy out of the World Cup final of 1966, but surely Geoff Hurst ended the argument with his historic hat-trick? Ask Sir Geoff who he regarded as the greatest English goalscorer of his lifetime then he'd have no hesitation in saying, "Greavsie". Jimmy had still got plenty of life left in him, being a national treasure who a recession couldn't devalue. There was only one Greavsie. It's a funny old life.

How many saw Jimmy's first game in a Tottenham shirt? There were 12,000 fans at Home Park for Plymouth Argyle reserves vs Tottenham reserves during 1961. John 'Cardiff' Williams – 'Cardiff' because Argyle had another John Williams, who was there first – almost marked him out of the game, restricting the great man, who'd just returned from Italy, to just a couple of touches but they were touches into the net.

Greavsie was in a young Chelsea side that opened Ashford Town's floodlights at the age of 17. One fan was as impressed with David Cliss. Whatever happened to him? John Williams said that he'd been out injured and was playing a few reserve games on his way back to fitness, speaking fondly of playing well against Jimmy, although still regretted that he scored twice.

Jimmy Greaves, who'd soon be taking to the stage for a 70th birthday theatre show & tour, was on his soapbox about the John Terry saga. The supreme goal-poacher came out of Dagenham to make his name with Chelsea and England, while Terry made the same journey from neighbouring Barking. Greaves, sounding more like Clare Short than a dyed in the wool Tory, had little sympathy for Fabio Capello's embattled captain but called for a sense of proportion:

"I was on Sky about my show and 2 lads with them were talking about Terry. I asked if they'd heard of the Chilcot Inquiry. They went, 'No'. I told them it was about a guy who took us to war in Iraq. We've lost hundreds of soldiers, 100,000 people have been killed but nobody in this country gives a toss. John Terry sleeps with some bird then everyone's up in arms. Yes, he was wrong to do it, I feel very sorry for his wife, who seems to have been overlooked in all this, but what's going on? The world's gone mad".

Politics wasn't on the agenda for Jimmy's special night at London's O2 Arena. What there would be was ribald humour, maybe including, he hoped, a gag about Terry & nostalgia for an age long before millionaire players, WAGs, rapacious agents, round-the-clock media coverage & intrusive sponsors became the norm. No one embodied the era better. From the late '50s to the early '70s, Greaves' scoring feats for Chelsea, Tottenham and England gave colour, excitement & genius to English football.

He netted a breathtaking goal for Spurs in 1965 against Man. Utd. Receiving the ball with his back to goal 30 yds out, with a marker breathing down his neck, Jimmy spun, slalomed through the defence then rounded the keeper before rolling it into the net, all in 8 secs. It'd be wrong to assume that Greaves lived in the past or to pigeon-hole him as consumed by despair over missing the World Cup final of 1966, being scarred by his battle with alcoholism a few years later. He addressed those old chestnuts but also defined his talent in terms of a science-fiction movie franchise, invoking a cast of characters from an Indian batsman to a Scottish jester. The sci-fi allusion came when Jimmy reflected that he'd been capable of bicycle kicks and flashing headers, as well as the art of dribbling. Had he felt that he'd been doing something extraordinary?:

"No, it was my job. That was that. I started doing it in the school playground. It's instinctive, natural. I've no idea how I scored the goal against United. If you thought about it, you wouldn't do it as well. Watch Roger Federer or Sachin Tendulkar & it's the same. Someone hurls the ball down at Tendulkar then in a split second he's moved his feet and with a flick of the wrist it's 4 runs. Have you ever seen the Stargate films? They go through this brightly lit ring into a parallel world or another dimension. When I came out on to the pitch at White Hart Lane, Wembley or wherever, I became a totally different person to how I was in the dressing room. I knew what I had to do & was confident I could do it. I wasn't necessarily that assured off the pitch. In a way, when I passed through that tunnel, it wasn't me any more".

Jimmy's gift led to a move from Chelsea to AC Milan during 1961, but despite 9 goals in only 12 games for the Rossoneri he didn't settle, soon coming home to join double-winners Spurs. "Folk ask if I expected that I'd win the championship there but it didn't occur to me that you had to win anything. I just wanted to play. Danny Blanchflower said that it was about glory rather than winning things and I'd go along with that. At the show, most of the guests on stage will be Tottenham people – Dave Mackay, Pat Jennings, Steve Perryman, Ossie Ardiles & so on, which says a lot".

Spurs had still to repeat the title triumph that Greaves missed out on, in contrast with their closest rivals' hoard of silverware under Arsène Wenger and George Graham. Wenger, he said "stole Tottenham's clothes & hasn't given them back yet". Thus it was perhaps surprising to hear Jimmy say that he didn't enjoy watching Arsenal: "They don't play directly enough. If it's played accurately, the long ball can be devastating, but I watched them against Man. Utd, who just got back behind the ball then said, 'If you want to fart about, you can, you're not doing us any damage'. Passing it around is all very well if you've got Messi, Xavi and Iniesta. Most clubs haven't got players like that so adapt accordingly. I remember John Beck's team at Cambridge Utd. Everyone moaned about kick-&-rush but they got a couple of promotions. I would've scored loads playing off Dion Dublin!"

Denis Law, his flamboyant contemporary at Old Trafford, was Jimmy's favourite striker, while George Best was the finest player that he faced. Ron 'Chopper' Harris was his toughest opponent, with Bobby Moore and Dave Mackay the best he played with at international & club level respectively. Greaves admired Wayne Rooney, who was "starting to show that he's a truly great player", and would like to have partnered Didier Drogba. "He's quick & as strong as an ox. I'd have said, 'Look, Didier me old pal, don't fall over. Knock 'em over. You and me will get 80 goals in a season'".

If Greaves could've stepped through the Stargate wormhole to make it happen he might also have tried to avoid the French tackle that cost him his place in the later stages of the World Cup finals of '66 & watch his vodka intake more carefully, although it was "a silly myth" that the 2 were connected, having scored a staggering 96 goals in the 3 seasons after '66. "Folk think I became an alcoholic because Alf Ramsey chose Geoff ahead of me. The drinking came much later. I was very pleased for the England boys, but I wanted to play. I don't particularly like watching football. I'm not someone who's in love with the game. I have an interest in it, but I don't know if I ever had a passion for it. I just loved playing".

Alf Ramsey's biographers suggested that the manager thought Jimmy unreliable and an individual rather than a team man. "I honestly don't know how he saw me. He was hard to work out. Big Jack Charlton reckons Alf hated him – said 'Hello' before his 1st cap then never spoke to him again for 7 years". Greaves thought that the success of Sir Alf's wingless wonders meant managers became "obsessed with work-rate & forwards tracking back, and that's when the fun went out of it".

Why had his drinking got out of control? "I feel it's a genetic thing that I inherited, which was brought to the surface by certain episodes. All I know is that the years from '74 to '78 were lost to me. When I went on They Think It's All Over, I said me & George Best were collaborating on a book about our lives in the '70s, 'so if anyone can tell us where we were, we'd be very grateful'. I don't know how I slid into it. I even found myself in a mental home for several months. One day, 28th February 1978, I just thought, 'I can't do this any more' and that was it. I haven't had a drink since. Long may it continue, though there's no guarantees".

That anniversary beckoned, as did the birthday bash, along with a 13-date tour, opening in Wolverhampton the following Thursday. The O2 show would feature jokes & reminiscences before Jimmy threw it open to the audience. At Crewe, one fellow asked whether he'd have scored more goals "if he hadn't been so lazy". An old Chelsea team-mate, Frank Blunstone who was present, sprang to Greaves' defence, wagging a finger while informing the questioner that "You don't score 5 goals against Wolves then 5 away to Preston if you're lazy".

Jimmy always liked a laugh, recalling like a naughty boy how he and Bobby Moore used to mimic Alf Ramsey, a fellow East Ender who'd taken elocution lessons. "Alf tended to forget himself, putting an 'h' on the start of words that didn't have them while taking it off ones that did". Although preferring Morecambe & Wise, The Two Ronnies and Ken Dodd to "the modern comics", he was greatly amused by Andy Parsons of Mock the Week fame, who when asked to suggest the question if the answer was 10%, came up with: "How much blood is there in Amy Winehouse's blood?"

Greaves had also studied the way Billy Connolly commanded the stage, creating an atmosphere in which everyday observations could be hilarious. "I'm not a stand-up comedian, more a story-teller. A raconteur!" His wife, Irene, could no doubt tell some tales, having married him during 1958, filed for divorce when his alcoholism took over, before taking him back, although she wouldn't be present: "She's never seen me. I couldn't perform in front of her. I'd be too embarrassed. It's a dreadful way to earn a living, isn't it?" Perhaps, but that John Terry gag would come in handy.

Height 5ft 8in. Playing weight: 10st 8lb.

Born East Ham, 20th February, 1940.

Scored on Chelsea debut at Tottenham in 1957, aged 17. Charles Buchan of the 'News Chronicle' wrote that it was "the finest 1st-ever League game by a young player that I've seen".

Goalscoring debut for England vs Peru during 1959.

Youngest player to score 100 League goals in 1960, aged 20 years 290 days.

Joined Milan for £80,000 during 1961, scoring 9 goals in 12 games before Tottenham manager Bill Nicholson bought him for £99,999. Netted with a spectacular scissors-kick against Blackpool on debut.

Scored 2 goals as Spurs beat Athletico Madrid 5-1 in the Cup-Winners' Cup final of 1963.

1st-choice striker going into World Cup finals of 1966 but injured then replaced by Geoff Hurst, who scored a hat-trick in the final against West Germany.

Joined West Ham in 1970 in part-exchange for Martin Peters. Finished 6th with co-driver Tony Fall in the London to Mexico World Cup Rally.

Retired from the Football League during 1971 with 423 goals in senior club games, 357 coming in 516 League appearances.

After facing up to alcoholism, Jimmy became a pundit for ATV in the Midlands then was paired with Ian St John on ITV show 'Saint & Greavsie' from 1985-92. He later became the television critic for TV-AM and a football columnist for 'The Sun' then 'The People' & worked as an after-dinner speaker. Jimmy went to Downing Street with the 'other' 11 members of England's 1966 squad in 2009 to be presented with a World Cup-winner's medal. "It's been my misfortune in life to be the guest of 2 socialist prime ministers, Gordon Brown and Harold Wilson", he said. A great-grandfather, approaching his 70th birthday, Greaves was preparing for a gala night & tour the following year.

Former England and Spurs striker Jimmy Greaves, 77, who'd been wheelchair-bound since having a massive stroke said: "I'm delighted to be remarried to Irene". She stated: "Jim did brilliantly. He was able to say most of what he needed to say & the reverend helped him when he couldn't. It was a lovely day, very poignant and very emotional for the children. When we turned around I said, 'Come on then, husband' then everyone roared with laughter".

Devoted Irene had been nursing Jimmy since doctors told him that he'd never walk again following the stroke that almost killed him. It struck during May 2015, while he was having a cuppa with his wife, putting him in intensive care for 6 weeks. Greaves had since been unable to move his legs despite 100s of sessions of private rehab treatment. The legend was initially afraid that he'd never be able to talk again after losing his speech.

Following the service at St John the Baptist Church in Danbury, Irene, 77, said: "Honestly, we'd never thought about remarrying – as far as we were concerned we were always married but a couple of months ago we decided we were going to do it again, so I don't know which date to do the anniversary on now. I'm probably going to stick to the original March date, because next year it will be diamond. We got hitched on a Wednesday 1st time round. We had to because Jim was playing football on Saturdays. I can't begin to tell you how many weddings I've been to on my own.

We went to the local church this time, just family – there's quite a lot of us, really – with our 2 daughters as witnesses and Reverend Clive Ashley was absolutely super throughout the planning then the day. It was so pleasant, such a nice little ceremony then we went off to a local restaurant & had a good time. The kids really had a good time and got stuck into the celebrations. Jim was offered a brandy but he wouldn't take it. He wanted a cigarette but I had to remind him that he couldn't smoke in a restaurant, so we'd have to go outside. It really wasn't the weather for it though".

There were no speeches at the reception but grandson Harry did raise a toast 'to Nan & Grandad' during the meal. Harry's dad, Andrew, said: "It was a very special day and great for all the family to witness mum & dad tying the knot. It was a lovely day for the children and the grandchildren." When Irene first wed Jimmy he was just at the start of his brilliant career, having turned professional at Chelsea the previous year in 1957. He was still 4th on the list of England's all-time leading goalscorers behind Wayne Rooney, Sir Bobby Charlton & Gary Lineker but his goals-to-games ratio was far superior to those above him on the list, with Greaves still being widely regarded as England's greatest ever goalscorer.

Irene said: "He's still the same as he was, not much different really. I don't think much will change but he's well looked after and he loved it when he went to White Hart Lane to see the old stadium & the new one being built and when he went to the training ground. He might go back to the training ground, he really enjoyed that & for him to go when the players are training one day, that would be really nice for him".

Norman Giller stated that Lionel Messi's performance in the Champions League was worthy of the greatest goalscorer that he'd ever seen. "If I was paid a pound for every time I was asked 'How good was Jimmy Greaves?' I'd have enough money to pay for the book I'm publishing about him, but at last I have somebody to point to then say: 'That's how Jimmy scored his goals'. Lionel Messi's rightly being lionised after his 4-goal demolition of Arsenal for Barcelona. The way he runs at defences - cunning running, I call it - the way he lies to them, the way he changes pace and direction, but above all the way he finishes, is pure Greavsie.

The close control is identical, the sudden acceleration, the ability to shoot with either foot, the same low gravity & perfect balance; it's all a flashback for me to 'Our Jim', who'd scored 170 League goals by the time he was Messi's age, 22. Lionel's netted 119, without violent interruption from defenders including 'Chopper' Harris, Norman 'Bites Yer Legs' Hunter & 'Anfield Iron' Tommy Smith. If you think my memory's deceiving me, go to YouTube to enjoy a feast, especially Jimmy's 1965 demolition of the Manchester United defence on the way to a goal that opened the Match of the Day titles until the dawn of colour television.

His most dazzling goals came when he was wearing a Chelsea shirt and playing with the gay abandonment of youth. Sadly, few of his Chelsea crackers were captured on film or tape, but ask anybody who was around at the time & they'll confirm that many of them were magical. Greaves scored the small matter of 124 League goals for Chelsea before he was 21. Later, he helped himself to 220 League goals for Tottenham then hung up his shooting boots by the time he was 31, after scoring an all-time record 357 First Division goals. Figuratively speaking, he was unbeatable.

The legend that is Diego Maradona has handed Messi his worshipped No10 shirt and it'll be all eyes on Lionel in South Africa. For his sake, I hope the World Cup doesn't deal him the same cruel hand that gutted Jimmy during 1966. He's never let me forget that I wrote in the Daily Express of July 30th, '66: 'My all-time idol is Jimmy Greaves, but Alf Ramsey mustn't change a winning team'. The myth has since been allowed to grow that being left out of the World Cup final team turned Greaves to the bottle. That, as Jim would say, is gollocks. He was already a black belt at drinking & his problems were caused by a chemical imbalance rather than anything to do with football matters.

I can just about remember being in drinking schools with the likes of really serious imbibers of the calibre of Dave Mackay, Alan Gilzean and Bobby Moore. They could all drink Jimmy under the table, but for medical as much as physical or psychological reasons it was Greavsie who emerged with the burden of alcoholism. In collaboration with his manager Terry Baker & my son, heir, partner and best friend Michael, I'm publishing a limited edition book called 'Jimmy Greaves At Seventy'. We're describing it as the most complete Greavsie story, which isn't an exaggeration, because nobody has written about Jimmy in his 7th decade before. Jimmy introduces and autographs the book, which he dedicates to his tribe of 12 grandchildren, 'So that they know I've not always been a fat old git with 2 new knees'.

After having appeared on Setanta's FA Cup final broadcast last year along with Ian St John, Greaves is on a nationwide tour performing his stand-up comedy act - 'I'm not sure whether it's my final farewell tour or me comeback, you'll have to ask my manager'. Jimmy has always done everything better than most folk on the planet, whether it's playing football, entertaining on TV or drinking - he hasn't touched a drop since 1978, but still refers to himself as a recovering alcoholic. Now he tells jokes better than most stand-up comedians & he gets standing ovations at every one of his shows. The Fat Old Git on Two New Knees is, as he would say, a legless legend".


The 80-year-old football legend Jimmy Greaves and Ron Flowers, the other surviving member of England's 1966 World Cup-winning squad not already honoured, had been awarded MBEs at the start of 2021. The pair were part of a star-studded New Years Honours list, which recognised over 1,200 folk. Greaves, who held the record for the most career goals scored in Europe's top 5 leagues with 366, until Cristiano Ronaldo overtook him in 2017, said:

"I'm deeply honoured to receive this recognition for services to football from Her Majesty The Queen", Jimmy said. Football has been my life, from the day I started kicking a ball around as a kid at home in Essex, to signing for Chelsea at 15, then to Milan, those wonderful 9 years at Spurs, then West Ham & later, my work in television and the media. There have been highs and lows, but it's a game I will always love & will always be part of me. I'd like to dedicate this award to Irene, my family and friends. Thanks for all your love & support".

The star suffered a stroke in May 2015, which left him wheelchair-bound, with severely impaired speech, needing care 4 times / day. Greaves was hospitalised during April 2020, when Tottenham announced that he was receiving treatment and awaiting test results. He was released from hospital soon after to recover at home with his wife, Irene. A statement from the club said that the illness wasn't another stroke, nor was it related to coronavirus. His net worth was reported to be c. £8.1 million

Tottenham & Chelsea led the tributes for their former player Jimmy Greaves, who'd passed away at the age of 81. A host of Spurs legends lined the pitch inside the Tottenham Hotspur Stadium as a minute's applause was held before the 2 teams kicked-off their derby. Martin Chivers, Steve Perryman, Micky Hazard, Paul Allen, Ossie Ardiles, Gary Mabbutt, Graham Roberts, Glenn Hoddle, Ledley King and Michael Dawson were all present. Spurs fans held aloft flags & banners during the applause to remember the club's record goalscorer.

Former Spurs and England striker Gary Lineker said: "Jimmy made a fabulous contribution to football, with an incredible goalscoring record. He was devilishly funny as well with his wit and personality, so charismatic, but on the field of play folk will remember him most. Those of us that are old enough to have witnessed his magnificence at times, he could score all sorts of goals & was a beautifully graceful footballer and a wonderful finisher.

For me, Jimmy was one of my heroes as well. Growing up watching him play we didn't have the number of games on TV that we now do but I managed to see him play a few times. I also was fortunate enough to meet him on many occasions when he was always affable, fun & hugely knowledgeable. He was a great personality, a wonderful footballer, a man with huge charisma and fun, so he'll be much missed".

On an emotional day across football grounds, West Ham, another of Greaves' former clubs, also held a minute's applause before their Premier League match against Man. Utd, as did Brighton & Leicester City. Players from all 6 teams wore black armbands for Jimmy, who still held the record for most goals in the English top flight with 357. Spurs captain Harry Kane, who's 2nd behind Greaves of the club's top scorers, said before facing Chelsea:

"1st and foremost our condolences to Jimmy's family & close friends. It's a sad one but hopefully a day we can celebrate. He played for Tottenham and Chelsea, so hopefully we can put in a great performance in his honour. Jimmy was an incredible player and goalscorer and a legend for club and country. It's frightening really how good a player he was. For someone like me to look at his numbers then one day to go on to break those numbers would be incredible. I got to meet him back in 2017 & it's just a celebration of him today".

Greaves began his career with Chelsea, where his 41 goals during the 1960-61 campaign remains a record in a season for the Blues. West Ham displayed images of their former striker around London Stadium as a minute's applause was held. Former Hammers team-mate Geoff Hurst was among those to pay tribute to Jimmy.

Jimmy Greaves was one of the finest strikers England has ever produced, but his legacy stretches far beyond the football pitch. As tributes poured in for the Chelsea and Tottenham legend, who'd passed away at the age of 81, his son revealed that the star spent his last day watching cricket surrounded by his wife, Irene & their 4 children. His loving family stuck by Jimmy through thick & thin as he battled a long-running alcohol addiction, which led to him 'losing a decade' to the bottle.

At a time when mental health was rarely discussed in sport, his fans rallied round after he bravely opened up in 1978 saying 'Drink is killing me'. Greaves stated that The Sunday People front page saved his life after a downward spiral towards drinking 12 pints and a bottle of vodka / day. While his alcoholism led to his marriage breaking down, Irene continued to support her man, the couple later tying the knot again during 2017 after a devastating stroke that left him struggling to say his vows.

Jimmy signed his 1st professional contract with Chelsea in the summer of 1957, for a miserly wage of £3 / week. To top up his income, he worked at a steel company that summer, also taking an office job for the club's secretary, John Battersby. Greaves recalled that the players would nip across to Charlies at lunchtime, a greasy spoon cafe: "They served a smashing plate of bacon, eggs, sausages, beans & fried bread. It was the sort of daily meal to make Arsene Wenger pale!"

By then he'd already met the love of his life, he and Irene getting hitched at a small registry office ceremony in Romford, Essex, during March 1958. Shortly afterwards, the couple had their first daughter, Lynn, but in 1961 they were left heartbroken by the tragic death of their son, Jimmy Junior. Greaves said that they were "inconsolable" after the baby died from pneumonia at just 5 months old. "There was no rhyme or reason about it. It just happened. He'd been a healthy baby, 9lb at birth then when he died we didn't speak about it - you were told to go home and get on with your lives. There was no counselling", stated Irene.

David Tossell, the author of 'Natural: The Jimmy Greaves Story', revealed that Jimmy's grief still haunted him years later when England lifted the World Cup during 1966. Despite being included in the squad, only players on the pitch in the final received medals, so the striker had to wait decades to be awarded one. Speaking about the tournament, Tossell said of Jimmy: "He once said 'Do you think I'm bothered about missing one game when I lost a 4 month old?'".

The star told the biographer: "Jimmy's death devastated us, it nearly drove us out of our minds. We were inconsolable, if ever there was a time in my life when I had wanted to call back yesterday, it was the day young Jimmy died. Though we still had Lynn, our grief lay before us, our joy seemingly behind us. You grieve for the death of any loved one but when it's for your own child no words can describe that grief".

After moving to Spurs, Greaves went on to become the club's highest goal-scorer of all time but after leaving the top flight in 1971, he struggled to adjust to life after football, opening up about the experience during 2003: "I think that a lot of players would prefer to have been shot once their career was over, because they've found it very difficult to battle through life. A lot of them never really find a substitute for football".

Turning to alcohol, he began drinking a bottle to 1 1/2 bottles of vodka, along with c. 12 pints of beer / day, often driving when over the limit: "I lost the '70s completely. They passed me by. I was drunk from 1972 to 1977". The addiction destroyed his marriage, with Irene forced to sell her jewellery to keep the family home. Unable to cope, the couple divorced in 1977, with Jimmy spending periods sleeping rough, selling women's jumpers in Wanstead after facing bankruptcy.

However, determined to turn his life around, Greaves made headlines across Britain when he opened up a year later: "I have to face up to the truth. If I carry on drinking I'll kill myself. I probably go through half a bottle of vodka before the pubs open in the morning then when the pubs open, I hit them. I drink beer in the pubs, not spirits then I carry on with vodka after they close. I'm a very sick man. I'm a social drinker who went off the rails, without realising it. I hope people will understand & have the compassion to realise that this is a serious illness".

Jimmy's pal Terry Baker said that he'd never -forgotten seeing his copy of the People plastered with the cry for help. Speaking after a feature-length documentary titled 'Greavsie', broadcast on BT Sport, Baker said: "I remember walking into my grandmother's house when I was a young man and seeing the front page story. It was heartbreaking, to me & loads of Jimmy's fans. Years later, when I got to know him really well, he told me that the story was going to come out anyway, so it was best that he did it himself.

He was pretty heartbroken that it was going to be in the public -domain. He hated the fact it had happened & he hated when it came out with all the publicity that surrounded it but he came to realise that it was the day that probably saved his life, because it really shocked him and he didn't want folk to know about the state that he'd got himself into. That was the day that woke him up & made him see sense".

Greaves and Irene remained close despite their divorce. The England star had moved out to a one-bedroom flat in Wanstead, but longed to reconnect with his family, who were living at his former home in Upminster. "Irene said that she didn't divorce me, she divorced the stranger I'd become. I was living in the flat but home is where the heart is and my heart was in a house on The Fairway in Upminster where Irene was living with our children".

After going for a final pint in Brentwood, Jimmy checked himself in to Warley Hospital to get treatment for his addictions. Promising Irene that he'd stay sober, she took him back, the couple living like husband & wife again. "We've been together 63 years now and we always considered ourselves married, even when we weren't. We still went out for our anniversary", Irene said.

Greaves had surgery on an artery in his neck following a mild stroke during 2012 then 3 years later, fans were sad to hear that he'd experienced a 2nd, more severe stroke, which left him unable to speak. In intensive care, his health slowly improved then after leaving hospital Jimmy continued his recovery in a wheelchair, before remarrying Irene in 2017 with a small service at a village church: He did brilliantly at the ceremony. He was able to say most of what he needed to say and the reverend helped him when he couldn't. It was a lovely day, very poignant & very emotional for the children".

Following a campaign by fans, Greaves received his long-awaited World Cup medal during 2009 due to a FIFA rule change then was awarded a MBE in the New Year Honours list of 2021, along with fellow World Cup squad winner of 1966, Ron Flowers, for services to football. On Sunday 19$^{th}$ Sept. of that year, it was announced that he'd passed away at the age of 81, leading to many tributes from the footballing world:

'We're extremely saddened to learn of the passing of the great Jimmy Greaves. We extend our deepest sympathies to Jimmy's family and friends at this sad time. Rest in peace, Jimmy', read Spurs' official Twitter account. Fellow ex-striker Alan Shearer wrote: 'RIP Legend. Goals, Goals, Goals. A remarkable goal scorer". Sharing a picture of himself with Jimmy, Spurs' striker & England captain Harry Kane wrote: 'RIP Jimmy Greaves. A true legend and one of the great goalscorers. Thoughts are with his family and friends'.

England announced plans to honour Jimmy, who'd been seriously ill for several years since having a massive stroke in 2015. He was survived by Irene, his 4 children, Lynn, Mitzi, Danny & Andrew, 10 grandchildren and his 5 great-grandchildren. Greaves spent his last day watching cricket surrounded by his wife, Irene & their children. His son Danny said:

"He was a big cricket fan and he watched the T20 Blast finals. We had the family – me, my brother, 2 sisters & mum – with him all the time, and thankfully he went very peacefully in his sleep, without any pain. There's a lot of sadness, of course, but the last 6-and-a-bit years since dad had his stroke have been tough, so on what's a very sad & upsetting day, you also know the pain and emotion of seeing him suffer & battle with it all the time has gone. With all of us, there's that relief that dad is comfortable now and wherever he is, he's happy".

Jimmy had his share of heartache, cruelly missing the World Cup final of 1966 after being injured & losing his 4-month-old son Jimmy Jr. He also battled alcoholism, which he said was "killing him" and cost him his marriage but he recovered to become part of football's favourite TV double act in Saint & Greavsie alongside pal Ian St John, having won his beloved Irene back.

Jimmy stated: "As parents, you expect your children to outlive you and when that doesn't happen, you become an empty shell. Jimmy was a beautiful boy and his time on this earth was all too brief. It kind of puts losing my World Cup winner's medal to Geoff into perspective, doesn't it, but you don't go through life without having some really bad times & I've had some great times, too. Jimmy's death devastated us, it nearly drove us out of our minds. We were inconsolable. You grieve for the death of any loved one but when it's for your own child no words can describe that grief".

Jimmy was friends with some of the greatest players of all time including Bobby Moore & George Best, having said of Best: "He was the first true modern footballer – the one every mediocre millionaire of the modern game should get down on their knees and thank. George was the ultimate showman. His attitude was 'Why simply beat a defender when you can torture him and entertain your public too?'".

Irene said: "He was 5 months old and there was no rhyme or reason about it. It just happened. He'd been a healthy baby, 9lbs at birth & when he died we didn't speak about it – you were told to go home and get on with your lives. There was no counselling. I've still got a lovely picture of him hanging on my wall with all the other family photos".

Greaves had been credited with encouraging thousands of folk to tackle their own alcohol abuse, having battled the killer disease for decades. He and Irene separated then divorced during his fight against alcoholism but reunited after 18 months then re-married at St John the Baptist church in Danbury, Essex on 7th September 2017. Irene said: "We've always adored each other, without a doubt".

She spoke of her torment dealing with his illness, saying: "I never wanted anyone else, but I look at him now & think he's not the man he was. I've lost my best mate. There was no one like him". She said that during the pandemic, carers came to their home 4 times / day to look after his basic needs: "They were fabulous. During lock-down they did the shopping, went to the chemists, doctors, everything. People love Jim. He's a thoroughly nice man and he's been incredibly generous. It's been an unconventional life but an amazing one, really".

Following his retirement from professional football, Jimmy Greaves turned to broadcasting, interviewing Mike Tyson during 1987. 'Iron' Mike - at just 21-years-old – gave a powerful performance with a flurry of ferocious punches. Jimmy stood in the ring as he questioned the 'Baddest Man on the Planet'. With an incredible 34-0 record – 30 of those via knock-out – there was no denying that Tyson was at the peak of his boxing career.

Greaves' asked him who was his favourite boxer, Mike saying: "My favourite fighter of all time – not probably the greatest - but my favourite fighter? I love Joe Louis". Tyson added that he thought the greatest fighter of all-time was Sugar Ray Robinson, saying that "he had everything".

Jimmy discussed Iron Mike's boxing technique, who gave an exhibition by one of the best ever boxers in his prime, demonstrating what he did best. Tyson commentated throughout saying: "I just punch with snap. My shoulders & my legs bring the punches together with accuracy and precision. The object of the game is when I hit the punch, boom, boom! Then I twist, I'm at the side, where you can't hit me", Mike explained, as he mauled Greaves into position.

Jimmy looked startled as Tyson demonstrated his technique, missing him by a very small margin, with explosive hooks that would most definitely hurt. "Yeah, I get the point!" exclaimed Greaves, who looked stunned after seeing Mike's devastating ability up close.

Jimmy Greaves' wife Irene, 81, said his award of a MBE in the New Year's Honours of 2021, was '20 years too late' & 'not a very good honour', believing that he deserved a knighthood. Greavsie, so secure was his place in the nation's heart that the fond nickname alone identified him, the greatest goalscorer in British football history, had belatedly been given the gong following a campaign, supported by the Daily Mail. Was it a fair acknowledgement of Jimmy's dazzling talent and contribution to football? Irene, who'd stood by him through triumph & tragedy, joy and sadness for over 60 years, thought not:

"The MBE is a small degree of recognition for him but it's 20 years too late & it's not a very good honour. I think he's worth more than that. He still holds all these records and he's done so many things in his life. Now he's 80, he's had a devastating stroke & they're finally doing something about it. I think they feel they've got to give him something to stop folk going on about it, but Jimmy really deserves a knighthood and I told him so. He seemed to agree. He said, 'Yes, yes', but if I mention it again he'll probably have forgotten all about it. I'm not too happy about it & I want to say what I feel. He won't decline it — he's a royalist — but I don't know how we'll get him to the Palace. It's not straightforward", she said from their home in the Essex village of Little Baddow.

Greaves, once so dazzling on the pitch, who had a 2nd career as a gloriously un-PC TV football pundit, was confined to a wheelchair, his speech slow and halting, his memory poor. For the past 5 years Irene hadn't left Jimmy's side for over an hour. "He cried when I told him about the MBE. Believe it or not, he had a small glass of wine, his 1st drop of alcohol since 1978, to celebrate". Had Greavsie then gone on a drinking spree? "No, he didn't!" she said with a laugh.

Irene was a strong woman, warm, funny & loyal, her love for Jimmy and his for her, having weathered vicissitudes that would've destroyed a weaker relationship. They wed in 1958 when they were both teenagers then lost a child, their first-born son, Jimmy Jr. at 5 months to cot death. Capable, forthright & hard-working, Irene trained as a nurse while raising their 4 other children — Lynn, 62, Mitzi, 59, Danny, 56, and Andy, 54 — during the dark days of Greaves' alcoholism.

"We've always adored each other, without a doubt. I never wanted anyone else, but I look at him now & think he's not the man he was. I've lost my best mate. There was no one like him. He was so charismatic, so funny. Now he's a shell of the man he was. After his last stroke I didn't think he'd make it and in a way I think it'd have been better if he'd gone. This is no life for him. He doesn't want to be here. He says: 'Get me something so I can go' & I tell him: 'You'll have us both in jail'. Sometimes I wish he could just slip away peacefully.

I know that's what he wants and although many folk have worse lives, as a carer you feel a bit trapped. My eldest daughter Lynn lives nearby & she's in my bubble, so she calls round quite a bit, but I can't leave Jim for more than an hour. Sometimes we have a tiff then I say: 'That's it. You're going into a home!' but I don't mean it, of course. I'd never, ever do that. I've promised the children I won't too. I'd never want that for Jim".

Those who followed the beautiful game, along with many who didn't, felt that they knew Greavsie, his affable appeal being universal. His strike-rate on the pitch remained unequalled in half a century, no one having surpassed his record-breaking tally of 357 goals in top-flight English football, for Chelsea, Tottenham Hotspur then West Ham but while other players were immortalised in statues or honoured with titles, Jimmy was overlooked.

In his heyday he'd be mobbed by girls wherever he went, Irene said, but she never worried about him straying. Life was simpler then. "Jimmy was only paid £17 / week during the '60s & £100 if he played for his country, but they were happy days and we weren't short of a bob or 2. We used to walk down to the Bell & Hare pub on Tottenham High Road after a game to have a drink with the supporters. They couldn't do that today, could they?

The money the players get now is obscene. No one's worth that much. They complain about the pressure but Jimmy would say: 'Where's the pressure in playing a game you love when you've got a natural talent for it?' and the WAG wars you read about, they both need to grow up really, don't they?" - The feud between footballers' wives Coleen Rooney & Rebekah Vardy was being waged in the High Court.

They were golden days but Greaves' had a setback in 1965, being diagnosed with infectious hepatitis. Showing huge determination, he regained fitness then was picked for the following year's World Cup squad, but a deep gash in his leg, inflicted during a winning match in the group stage against France, cost him his place in the rest of the tournament. Although Jimmy was match-fit by the time England made the final, manager Alf Ramsey stuck with Geoff Hurst, who scored the hat-trick that led to England's historic win against West Germany. Only those who played in the final received medals:

"Today they have substitutes but in those days they didn't. They had 11 players on the pitch and that was it, so Jimmy wasn't even on the bench. All my life I've hated Alf Ramsey for it. Totally illogically, I know, but it was dreadful at the time for us. We went off on holiday very quickly afterwards. It should've been Jimmy's crowning glory but I think he got over it more easily than I did", said Irene.

Had it led to his alcoholism? "I think the drink problem would've come anyway. Jimmy has always said that it wasn't disappointment or the pressure of playing in the top flight that caused the problem, but more the void left to fill when the structure, rigour & discipline of training lessened. He also felt snubbed when, despite scoring a record 266 goals for Spurs, he was told that his services were no longer required at the club then he was sold to West Ham".

At about this time Greaves' drinking escalated then by the early '70s he was an alcoholic. "He'd just shut himself away in a room at home and drink. I just got fed up with him. I realised that it was no good nagging or pouring his drink down the sink, because he'd hide bottles everywhere. I had to wait until he was ready to stop himself. He'd promise to give up but he carried on. I'd say to him: 'You'll drink yourself to death & you won't be here to see the kids grow up', but nothing worked, so we divorced. I told him to go. He moved out into a flat and I trained as a nurse while looking after the children". Irene went on to work as a practice nurse at their local GP surgery for 13 years.

"Andy, our youngest, was about 10 at the time, but 18 months later Jimmy came back home. He said: 'I'm ready to give up drinking now' — and I just knew he meant it this time. Lynn drove him to Warley Hospital - for psychiatric patients - in Brentwood. He'd been there twice, unsuccessfully, but it was 3rd time lucky. There was a small pub on the corner. He went there to have his last pint of beer then that was it. He stopped. That's the strength of the man, really. We'd have drink in the house & he'd pour me a wine, before he had his stroke of course, but he never touched it again until he had that one glass to celebrate his MBE".

They moved to their latest home — "It's a lovely place to live, surrounded by National Trust woodlands", as Greaves' began his 2nd successful career as a TV football pundit. He was a natural, bringing his own brand of relaxed joviality to the screen, so when he teamed up with fellow former footballer Ian St John to discuss the day's matches, their ITV show — Saint And Greavsie — was a hit:

"Everyone loved it. He'd say cheeky things, very un-PC, which I don't think would be allowed today. They were all off the cuff, because he's a bit dyslexic, so couldn't read the auto-cue, he'd ad-lib, just say what he wanted". When a new breed of sharp-suited broadcaster arrived during the early '90s, replacing convivial banter with crisp, forensic analysis, Jimmy retired to a life of dog-walking, armchair sport & the companionship of his beloved Irene. "If he watches sport on television now, it's normally cricket and rugby. He very rarely watches football. He reckons they can't play anyway".

They remarried in 2017, with a small ceremony in their village church. "Oh, it was a lovely day. We've been together 63 years now & we always considered ourselves married, even when we weren't. We still went out for our anniversary". Irene thought Greavsie's era of football was the best. "We were never millionaires but Jim made a good living. He loved what he did and sometimes I think he'd have done it for nothing. People love Jim. He's a thoroughly nice man & he's been incredibly generous. It's been an unconventional life but an amazing one, really".


Football legend Jimmy Greaves said he was feeling "lucky to be alive" after having a devastating stroke, collapsing at home during April 2015. The 75-yr-old fought back tears as he said he'd been given a 2nd chance at life. Jimmy gave the thumbs-up, declaring that he was determined to get back to his best : "I should be dead, but I'm here and I'm fighting fit. Now I want to live until I'm at least 90. Hopefully there's a few years left in me yet. I've promised my grand-kids that I'll go to watch them play rugby & hockey when they go back to school, so I've got to get better".

Greaves was sitting in a black wheelchair in hospital when he spoke about his near-death ordeal, with his caring sons Andy and Danny by his side, still clearly struggling to cope with his life-changing stroke 8 weeks earlier. It took away all feeling in his famous feet & made speech very difficult. Jimmy had been worried that he'd never talk or walk again but had regained the feeling in his limbs and his ability to converse. For weeks he'd to use a notepad to communicate with doctors & his beloved wife Irene, 75.

The former England, Chelsea, Spurs and Hammers star was still unable to stand or use his right arm, relying on relatives to help him communicate but while the stroke might have taken away his once free-flowing speech, it had left his razor-sharp mind & famous wit undimmed. Greaves joked that it was only after falling ill that Irene realised quite how much he did around the house, adding that he'd been asking his family to sneak in a McDonald's for him.

After just a few minutes with Jimmy, who was in a rehab centre, it was clear that he was determined not to let the stroke beat him, saying: "I'd like to be a bit better but I'm taking every day as it comes and I'm feeling good. I'm much better than I was. I'm getting my speech back & I can move my right leg now. I haven't got any feeling in my right arm but my left arm and hand are absolutely fine so I can still sign my autograph perfectly. I'm a long way from being back to my best & I don't know whether I can ever get back to it, but I'm determined to do everything I can. I'm a fighter. Every day is a new day. The doctors reckon after a year if something isn't working it'll never work. I've got another 9 months until then and I've come on a lot already, so hopefully it'll come".

Greaves still vividly remembered the moment on May 3rd when the stroke hit : "When I had the stroke I was dying really. It was c. 8.30am & I was sitting having a cup of tea with Irene in our living room. I knew something was wrong, because I started to have chest pains and I was feeling unwell. I went down then crashed out. That's the last thing I remember until I woke up in hospital, but I know Irene rang 999, I was taken to A & E then put into intensive care. I woke up in hospital and just thought, 'I'm still alive'. I knew what had happened to me immediately. Blimey did I know. It was touch & go whether I'd survive for the first week but they saved my life. I was in intensive care for 6 days and I wasn't conscious".

In time Jimmy began to rally, at first being unable to talk or write at all but over the past few weeks he'd been taking steps towards his recovery: "I suppose the start of it was probably the worst really. I know now I wasn't up to it but in the 1st couple of days I was trying to get to my phone to do my column for the paper. It was very frustrating at first, because I was all there mentally and knew what was going on straight away but I couldn't communicate.

I was having to write everything down on a notepad for folk to read. I started to drink again after about a week, just water & cups of tea. I haven't had any alcohol for 37 years but my sons have said that I might need a beer after all this. I think they will too. I was on the front of the Sunday People in the '70s speaking about my alcoholism. I think doing that saved my life".

Doctors at Broomfield Hospital, Chelmsford, Essex, had begun to see an improvement in Greaves, who joked: "They said that they knew I was feeling a lot better when I told them that I wanted a burger and chips a couple of weeks ago. I asked for a quarter pounder from McDonald's but the doctors said it had too much bread, so my sons got me an ordinary cheeseburger & chips -instead. I get up at 6am for breakfast then I start the day. All of my family have been to see me and I've spoken to my nephew who lives in Australia on Skype. He wanted to come back but I told him not to.

I've been watching the cricket & the horse racing with my sons but we haven't had any winners at all. I'm having 5 hrs of therapy / day. I have physio. then speech therapy then I have electro therapy, when they put electrodes into my arms. Looking back 2 months from where I was, I'm much better now. It's not perfect yet but my speech has come on in leaps and bounds. I couldn't get a word out until 4 weeks ago but I can now. It's a massive step forward. The doctors say the left side of my brain hasn't been affected at all. There's a lot of hard work ahead, but I'll do everything I can to get back to where I was.

Hopefully I'll be able to go home in a couple of weeks. I'm ready to be out. I want to get home to Irene & my dog Lester. I know my recovery will progress even faster then. There's a meeting at the hospital next week to decide when I can go home. Irene has joked that she never realised how much I did around the house till now. She thought I didn't do anything. I want to thank all the doctors and nurses at the Broomfield Hospital. They've been great since day one. I've been touched by all of the messages of support. I've had more than 150,000. It's unbelievable. I just want to thank everybody".

Former team-mates, ex-TV colleagues & fans had sent their best wishes to Jimmy. There'd been messages from rock star Spurs fan Phil Collins, 64, TV host friend Ian St John and fellow 1966 World Cup winning squad members Sir Geoff Hurst, 73, Roger Hunt, 76, Gordon Banks, 77 & George Cohen, 75. England legends Gary Lineker and Peter Shilton had also sent Greaves messages of support.

Liverpool legend Ian St John, 77, who'd phoned every week, said: "Me & Jimmy had a great time when we did our tour a few years ago. Jimmy was one of the funniest men I've ever seen on the stage. I'm so pleased he's getting better". After retiring from football, Greaves went on to present Saturday lunchtime football programme Saint and Greavsie from 1985 to 1992 with Ian.

Sir Geoff, who scored a hat-trick in England's 4-2 World Cup final win over West Germany in 1966, said: "Me & Jimmy have been friends for 40 years. We've always been the best of friends and I'm rooting for him. Jimmy was the greatest goal scorer of mine and any lifetime & I'm desperately hoping he'll be well. If anyone can recover from this it's him". Phil Collins, who'd sent a couple of bouquets of flowers to Greaves' wife Irene, said: "Jimmy was my boyhood hero. I think about him regularly and I have a picture of him on my wall. I'm so happy he's improving."

Greaves was due to be inducted into Spurs' Hall of Fame on May 13th, ten days after having his stroke. Stroke Association chief executive Jon Barrick said: "We were deeply saddened to hear of Jimmy Greaves's stroke & wish him well in his recovery. It's an incredibly cruel condition that strikes in an instant with consequences that can last a lifetime. We're here for everyone whose life has been changed by stroke. Each step towards recovery is a victory". There are 152,000 strokes / year in the UK, being the 4th single largest cause of death but there are c. 1.2 million survivors.


Who was the greatest player that Jimmy played with during his career?

"A toss up between Dave Mackay and Bobby Moore. Dave motivated everybody around him with his inspirational performance. He could tackle like a tank, had an excellent left-foot cross-field pass that could change the direction of play and he never ever accepted defeat until the final whistle. Bobby Moore read the game better than anybody I've ever seen & was always in the right place at the right time. He wasn't the quickest thing on 2 feet, but was always yards ahead of the opposition in his thoughts".

Did Greaves have any memories of playing at Brighton and Hove's Goldstone ground? What did they need to do to get back in the big time?

"I only ever played at the Goldstone in a testimonial for either Alan Mullery or Bobby Smith. You need huge financial backing & lots of luck to get back to the Jimmy Melia Wembley days".

Could one really compare David Beckham to Bobby Moore and did Jimmy think that the former deserved to have the same standing in the game?

"You can't compare my great mate Mooro with David Beckham. One was a world-class defender, the other a midfielder-winger at various times. You can't compare eras, but both have done brilliantly in their careers".

What was the best moment of Greaves' career?

"There was a lot of pressure on me when I made my debut for Tottenham after moving from AC Milan in controversial circumstances. I silenced the critics by scoring a hat trick in a First Division match against Blackpool, including a scissor-kick goal that was as spectacular as any I ever scored".

How had it felt to miss out on the World Cup Final of 1966?

"Naturally I felt sick, but in Alf Ramsey's position I'd probably have done the same thing. The team played magnificently in the quarter & semi-finals, so Alf decided not to change a winning team. I had stitches in a gash on my shin following the 3rd match against France and that's what cost me my place in the side. Despite what people say, I never held a grudge against Alf. He had my respect as one of the greatest football tacticians of all time".

Had Jimmy got any regrets?

"My only 2 major regrets were missing the World Cup final & failing to get into the 1962 European Cup final with Spurs after I had a perfectly legitimate goal ruled off-side".

Which club had Greaves enjoyed playing at the most?

"I had equal satisfaction at Chelsea and Tottenham, but if you put a gun to my head I'd have to say Spurs, where I was more in control of my game & playing in a better side. At Chelsea I was just a kid playing it off the cuff without fear".

Who were the latest best players?

Steven Gerrard is the nearest thing that I've seen to the late, great Busby Babe Duncan Edwards. Cristiano Ronaldo is outstanding, but not in the class of George Best. I wish he wouldn't go over so easily. Michael Owen is the best goal poacher of recent years, and it's a pity he's had so many injuries. Wayne Rooney is exceptional, but needs to show that he has a good temperament to go with his talent".

How had Jimmy's stage career compared with TV?

"I like travelling the country with the road show - I get an instant feedback reaction from the audiences, which you don't enjoy on television. I loved every moment of my TV career, but that's history now. I know I'm biased, but I don't think there's a sports show on the screen to rival the old Saint & Greavsie programme. I know that makes me sound like a grumpy old footballer, but anybody who used to switch on to us in our peak years will, I believe, agree with my opinion".

One man's greatest opportunity was his friend's greatest disappointment and the lives of Sir Geoff Hurst and Jimmy Greaves had been bound together for 54 years thanks to one twist of World Cup fate. 'In terms of being intertwined it's as close as you could get,' said Hurst, who led the campaign to finally get a gong for Greavsie:

"All because of that one instance. Jimmy was injured against the French, so somewhat luckily I made my debut in the quarter-final. We did well, I performed well, so he struggled to get back in. It happens in all sorts of sports when one person replaces another. I've always thought I took my opportunity because I hadn't been disappointed to be left out at the start of the World Cup, when I was competing with Jimmy & Roger Hunt.

Jimmy was bitterly disappointed but not for one second was that feeling shown on a personal level. The question would often come up when we did theatre shows or the Q&As about whether Jimmy and I still got on, or whether there was any animosity over what happened on that day. There wasn't & there never will be".

Geoff scored the only goal of England's quarter-final against Argentina then 3 in the final against West Germany. He still had his unique place in footballing history as the only player to score a hat-trick in the World Cup Final. The honours followed: a MBE during 1979, being followed by a knighthood in 1998 , his life having since been defined by those few weeks during the summer of '66. A statue of Hurst with Bobby Moore, Martin Peters and Ray Wilson stood at the end of Green Street, near the old West Ham ground in Upton Park.

Geoff was about to record a sketch for Sport Relief about VAR & his 2nd goal in the World Cup final, the one which crashed off the bar then down on to the line at Wembley, being awarded after the referee consulted with the 'Russian linesman', Tofiq Bahramov, who was really from Azerbaijan. Hurst may have scored the most famous hat-trick but no one has scored more England hat-tricks than Greaves, the master finisher.

However, there'd been no formal honours for Jimmy and no statue, Geoff being determined to lead the 'Gong for Greavsie' campaign, which was launched earlier that year. There was an overwhelming reaction from newspaper readers, not just Spurs fans, over 32,000 having signed an on-line petition in support of the campaign:

"It's important that Jimmy is remembered by this generation & future generations as the great player he was. It's our sporting heritage, it's our national game, it's the world game and you're talking about the greatest goalscorer we have ever seen. He was a genius at doing one of the hardest things in the game: putting the ball in the back of the net.

He did it at a time when the game was physically much more violent than we see today & he started at Chelsea with a team predominantly in the middle of the table. We're not talking about Cristiano Ronaldo and Lionel Messi, who've done it with the 2 teams who've dominated in Spain and are beating teams 4, 5 & 6 nil. In his England games, at the top level where it was tough, his ratio is better than anybody's, 44 in 57, it's fantastic. There's no argument in football terms", said the 79-year-old Hurst.

Greaves was back home after a health scare earlier that year, which required a short time in hospital. The 80-yr-old had been confined to a wheelchair since a severe stroke 5 years earlier, which had limited his vision and speech & robbed him of the quick wit and sense of mischief that had endeared Jimmy to his armchair audience when he returned to the public eye in the '80s as a TV pundit & presenter, having overcome the perils of alcoholism.

'He was always a cheeky little imp. At schoolboy level he'd predict how many goals that he'd score, like Muhammad Ali when he forecast the knock-out round. He's always had this carefree attitude and it was linked to his success as a goalscorer. In golf you miss a putt then the next hole comes along & the poor players are still thinking about the putt that they missed. With Jimmy, if he missed that was gone. He once missed a penalty for Spurs against us. He knocked it over the top then came back to the halfway line and we knew each other well enough at the time to talk during the game. 'Geoffrey,' he said, 'sometimes they go in & sometimes they don't'. In the nicest possible way, he couldn't give a damn. That was his character", said Hurst.

Greaves would only play 3 times more for England after the World Cup of 1966. What should've been his finest moment had become the greatest disappointment of his career. His final match was a friendly against Austria in Vienna, during May 1967, when he played up front with Hurst. Alan Ball scored the only goal. The pair became team-mates again when Jimmy joined West Ham in March 1970 as part-exchange in Tottenham's signing of Martin Peters.

'He was probably slightly past his best but it was enjoyable. It was a great start. We scored 2 goals each on his debut, a famous game back in the days when we could go up to Manchester City and win 5-1. Ronnie Boyce volleyed the other one straight into the net from a kick by their goalkeeper, Joe Corrigan. I've a great picture of Jimmy & me, which was taken in that game. One of us had scored, we're congratulating each other and we're absolutely caked in mud from head to toe, as usual in those days.

So Jimmy was still scoring goals. Maybe not as many as he had been doing but don't forget he was in the Chelsea first team at 17. In those days if you were a striker as brilliant as he was, you'd probably expect to be finishing your career at around the age he was, which was 31. I'm not sure if he'd started drinking. I never knew he was a drinker or an alcoholic. I only found out when I read it in the newspaper when it dropped as a front-page story. I'd never heard any rumours about his problems", stated Geoff.

Greaves retired during 1971 after little over a year at West Ham then Hurst departed the following year to join Stoke for £80,000. "I wasn't as close to him as Mooro — they were room-mates — but I enjoyed his company. After we finished playing, I enjoyed seeing him from time to time & I enjoyed being on his theatre shows. He's someone that I've admired tremendously as a player and as a person. He was always a smashing guy to be with, just brilliantly funny", said Hurst.

Jimmy Greaves' former team-mate Sir Geoff Hurst, paid one of many tributes for Spurs' goal-scoring hero, who'd died at the age of 81 after years of fighting dementia: "Greaves was the best English forward ever. There were some great players, but the forward was judged by the goal & no one could touch him. I'm asked if there was hostility between Jimmy and me because I'd replaced him, but not for a second. You hear the word genius & that's one word that applies to Jimmy. He's certainly worth including on the list of England's best players, given his position as one of our biggest goal scorers and his role in the success of the 1966 World Cup".

Spurs and England striker Harry Kane paid tribute to "A true legend & one of the great goal scorers". Arsenal legend Ian Wright said that he was inspired to emulate Greaves when he was young: 'The name of the first soccer player I heard from my teacher. 'It's not Ian. End it like Jimmy Greaves', rest in peace," he tweeted.

From England manager Gareth Southgate, who said that there'd be a tribute paid to Jimmy when the team played against Hungary in Wembley the following month: "Jimmy Greaves was praised by everyone who loves football, regardless of club loyalty. Last year, when the club celebrated his 80th birthday at Tottenham Hotspur, it was an honour to meet Jimmy's family. My thoughts are with them and the whole game mourns his death. I know that".

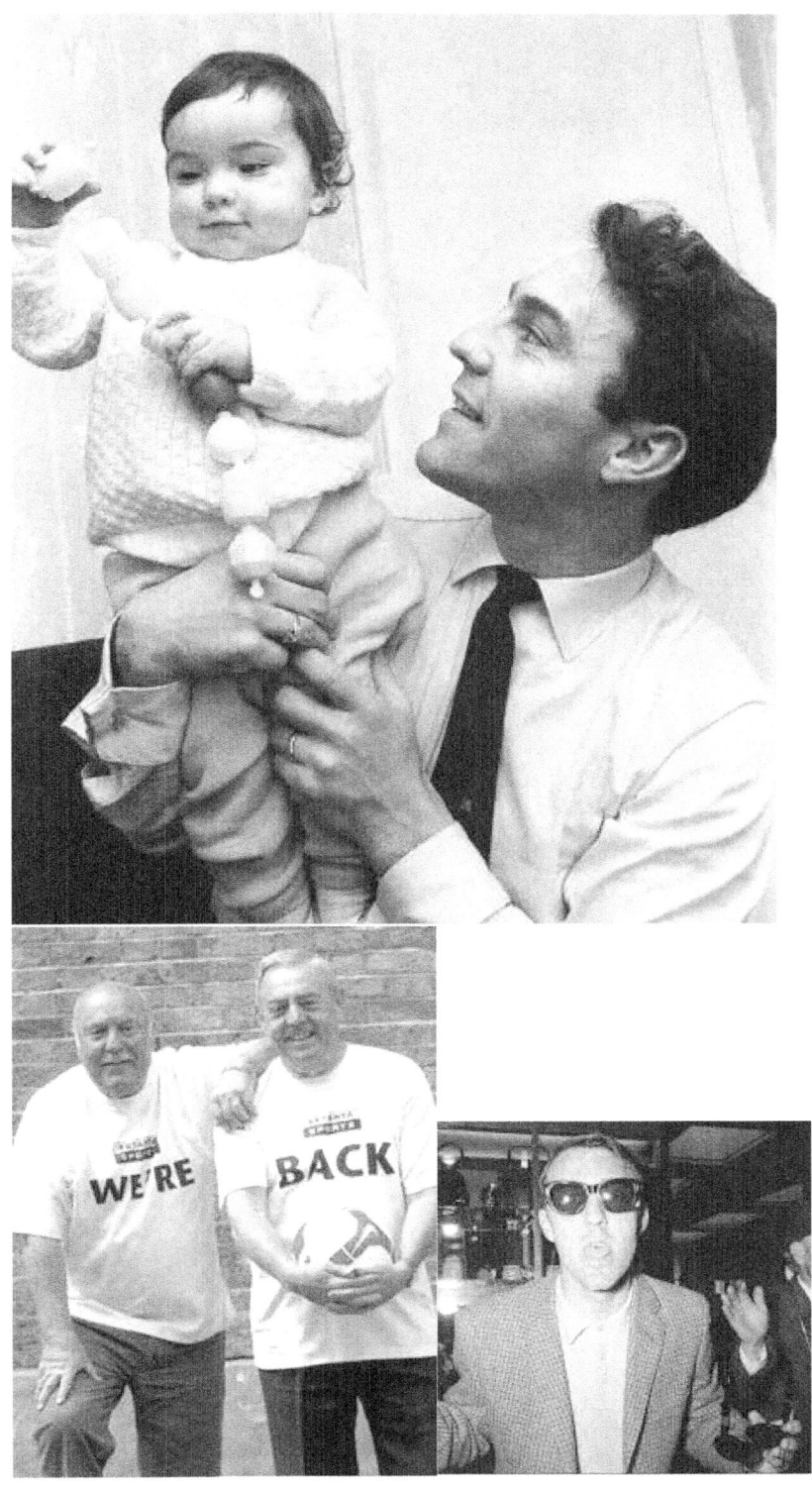

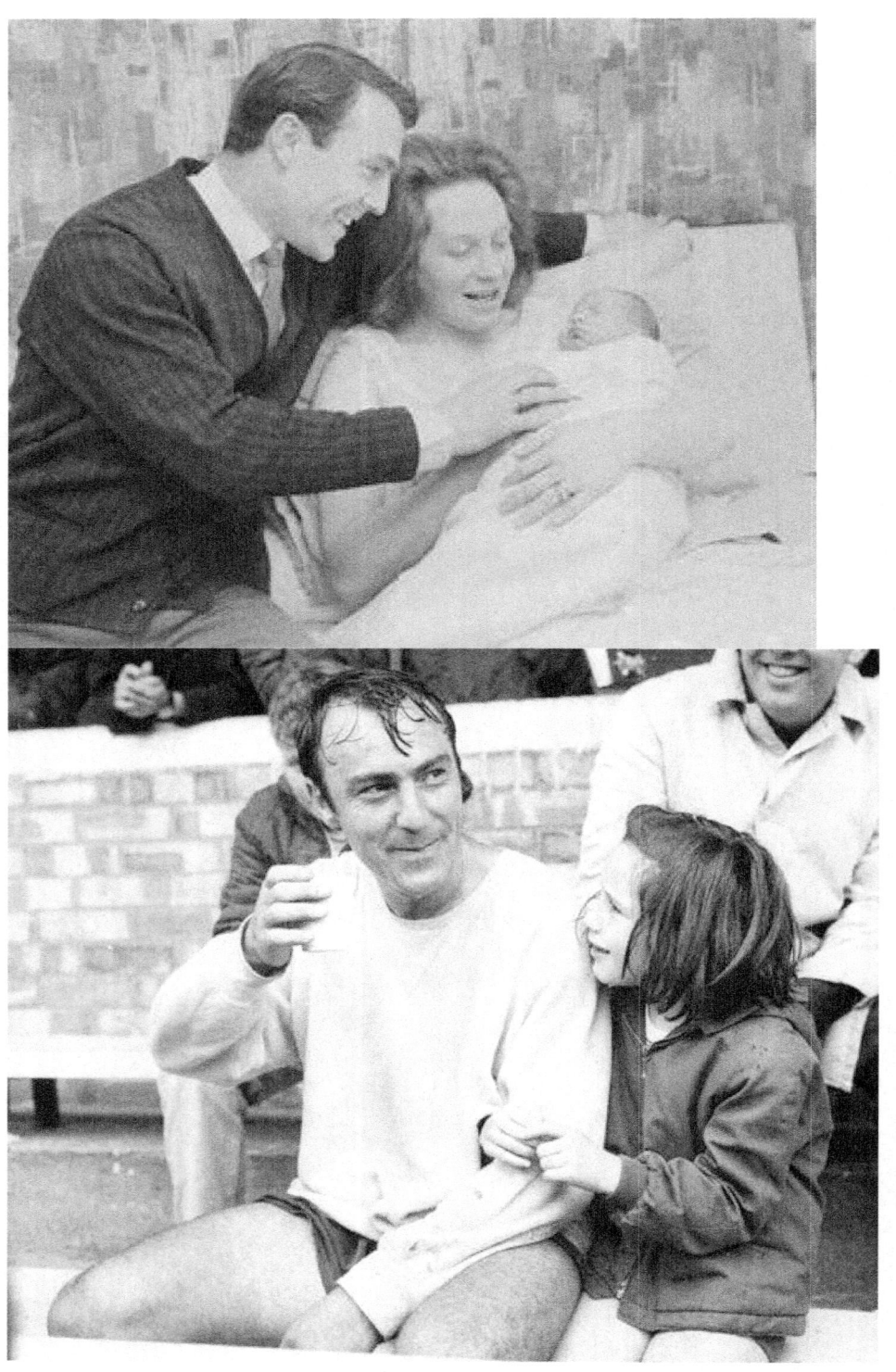

78

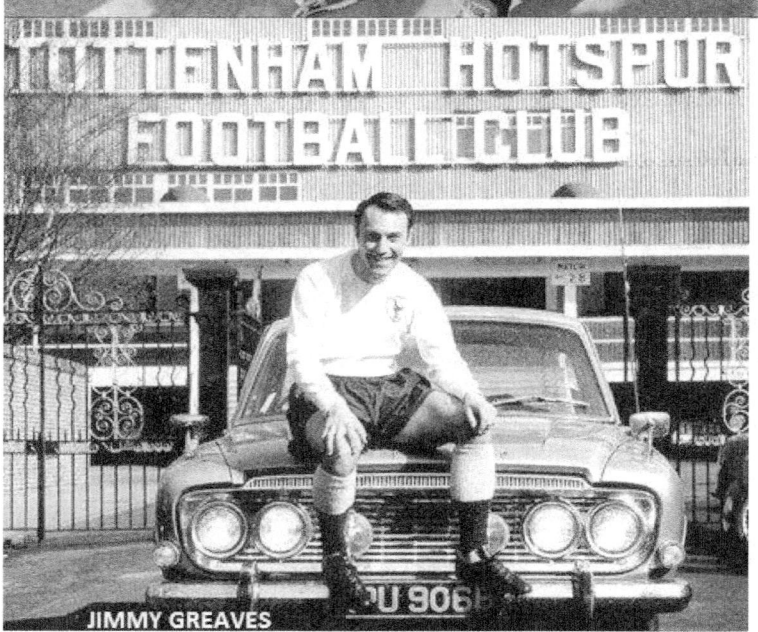

JIMMY GREAVES

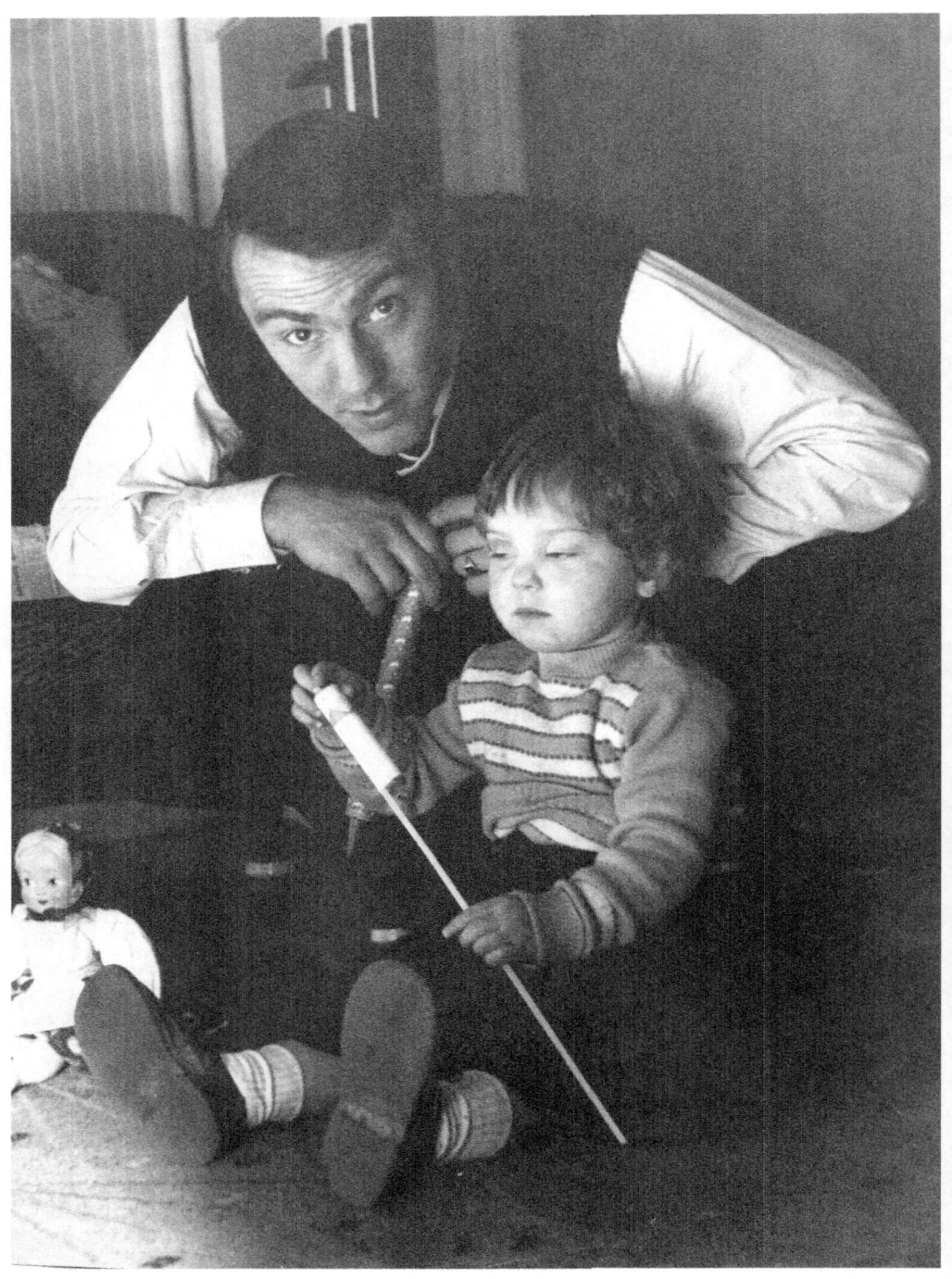

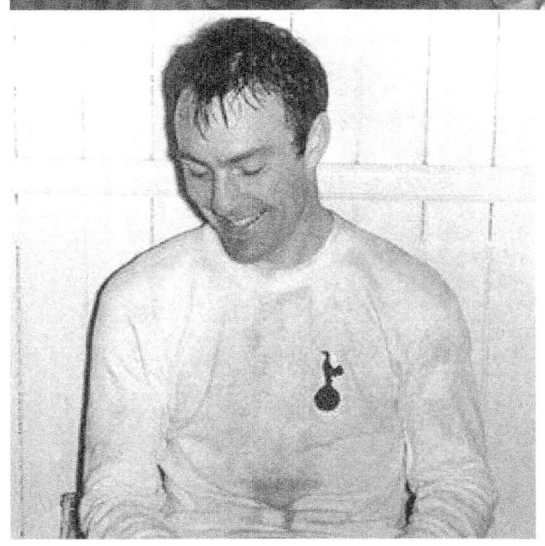

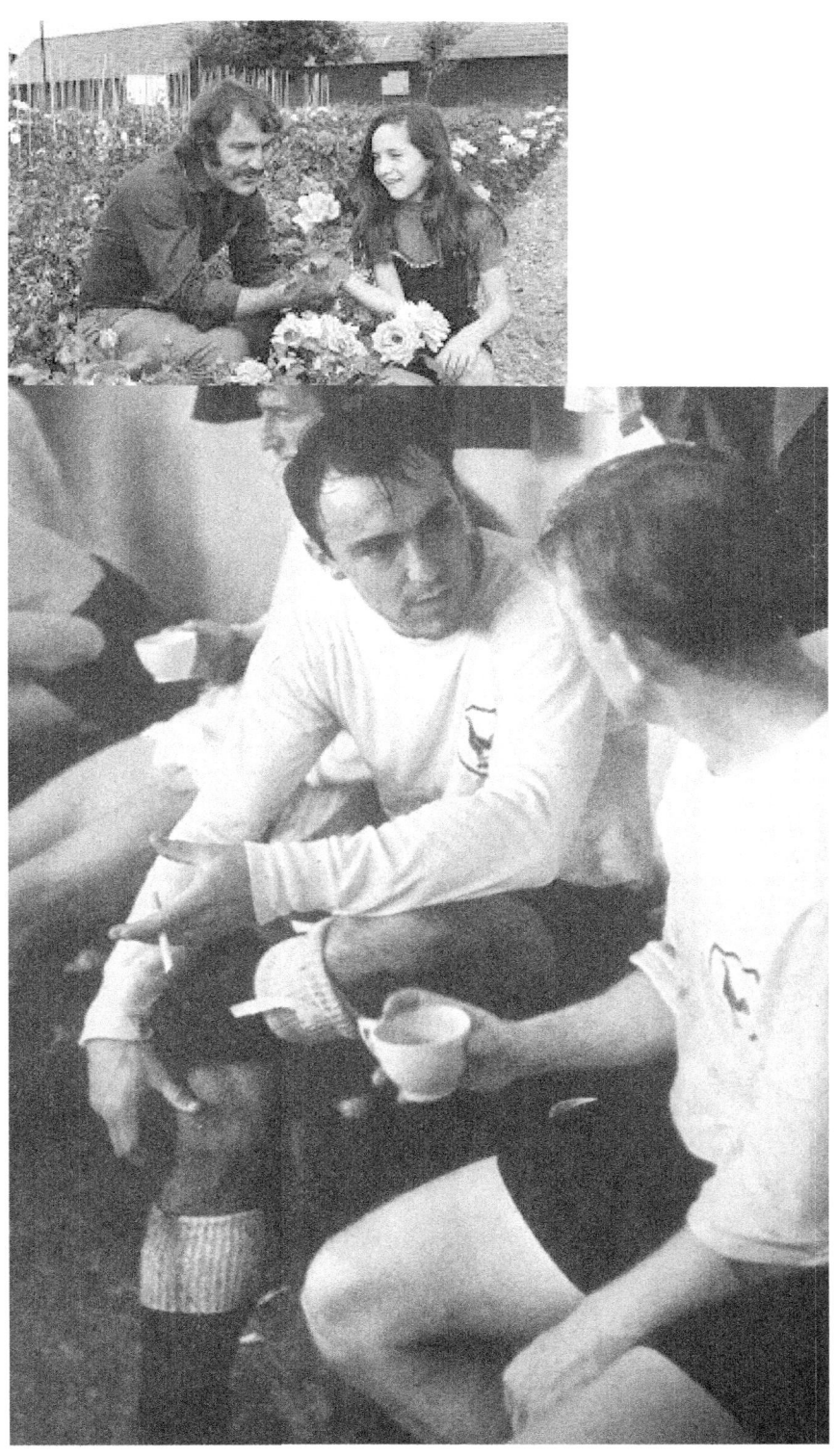

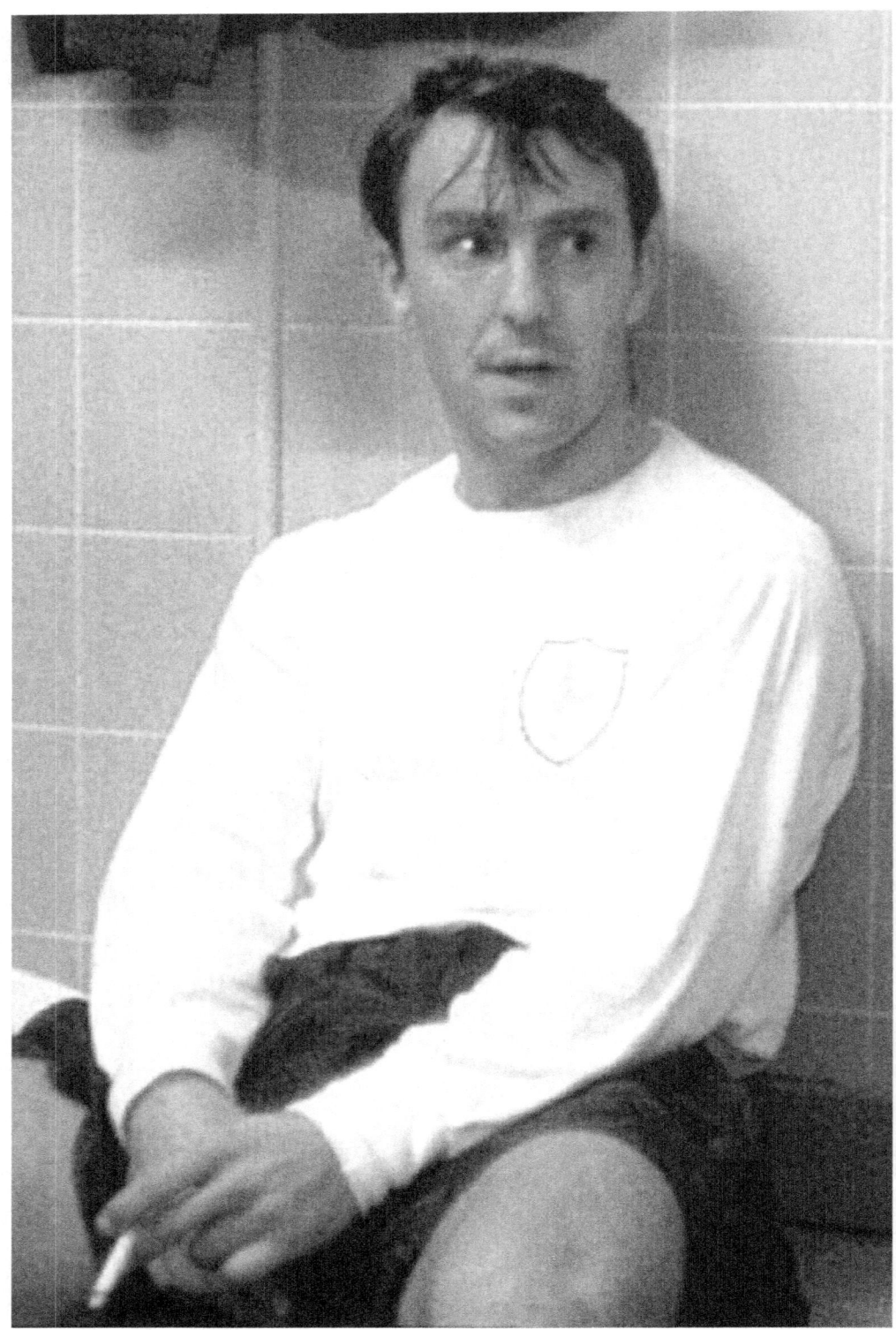

Printed in Great Britain
by Amazon

19861219R00068